On Who Is God?

A Book You'll Actually Read

Also available in the series:

A Book You'll Actually Read

On Who Is God?

Mark Driscoll

CROSSWAY BOOKS

WHEATON, ILLINOIS

On Who Is God?
Copyright © 2008 by Mark Driscoll

Published by Crossway Books
      a publishing ministry of Good News Publishers
      1300 Crescent Street
      Wheaton, Illinois 60187

Interior design and typesetting by Lakeside Design Plus
Cover design and illustration by Patrick Mahoney
First printing 2008

Printed in the United States of America

Scripture quotations are from *The Holy Bible, English Standard Version*®, copyright © 2001 by Crossway Bibles, a publishing ministry of Good News Publishers. Used by permission. All rights reserved.

All emphases in Scripture quotations have been added by the author.

Trade Paperback ISBN: 978-1-4335-0136-4
PDF ISBN: 978-1-4335-0446-4
Mobipocket ISBN: 978-1-4335-0447-1

Library of Congress Cataloging-in-Publication Data

Driscoll, Mark, 1970–
    On who is God? / Mark Driscoll.
      p. cm.—(A book you'll actually read)
    Includes bibliographical references (p.   )
    ISBN 978-1-4335-0136-4 (tpb)
    1. God (Christianity) 2. God. 3. Christianity and other religions. I. Title.
II. Series.

BT103.D75   2008
231—dc22

                                                              2008000483

VP	16	15	14	13	12	11	10	09	08
	9	8	7	6	5	4	3	2	1

Contents

Series Introduction

On Who Is God? is part of an ongoing series of books you will actually read. The average person can read these books (minus the appendixes) in roughly one hour. The hope is that the big truths packed into these little books will make them different from the many other books that you would never pick up or would pick up only to quickly put down forever because they are simply too wordy and don't get to the point.

The A Book You'll Actually Read series is part of the literature ministry of Resurgence, called Re:Lit. Resurgence (www.theresurgence.com) is a growing repository of free theological resources, such as audio and video downloads, and includes information about conferences we host. The elders of Mars Hill Church (www.marshillchurch.org) have generously agreed to fund Resurgence along with the Acts 29 Church Planting Network (www.acts29network.org) so that our culture can be filled with a resurgence of timeless Christian truth that is expressed and embodied in timely cultural ways. Free downloads of audio and/or video sermons by Pastor Mark Driscoll on topical issues and entire books of the Bible are available at www.marshillchurch.org.

Introduction

"In God we trust"—that's what our money says. However, if you were to randomly ask the people handing their money to the checkout clerk in your local grocery store, "Who is God?" it is doubtful they would be able to clearly articulate who this God is. Our predicament is not unlike the experience of Paul when he walked into the great city of Athens only to discover that it was littered with memorials to an unknown god.[1] We would say that they were very spiritual people.

Paul responded by proclaiming that Jesus was the God they were ignorant of and that they needed to worship him alone. Because the Athenians had not previously heard of Jesus, they brought Paul before the Areopagus ("Mars Hill" in Greek), which was the high court of Athens that evaluated any new ideas promulgated in the city. Standing on the same ground where Socrates had defended himself 450 years earlier, Paul clearly articulated who God is and what he has done through the death and resurrection of Jesus.

In many ways, much of our culture is very Athenian. Most people believe in God but, like the Athenians, they are uncertain who God is or how to come to any informed certainty. My hope is that this little book will help fill a need somewhat like Paul did

1. Acts 17:16–34.

on Mars Hill, though admittedly without the same degree of authority since this little book will never make it into the Bible.

The research for this book began when I was a college freshman, a spiritual person who thought there was a God but had no idea who that God was. As I studied, my questions were answered, and I became a Christian at the age of nineteen. Within six years I went on to be a pastor and plant a church that attracted many mainly non-Christian young, hip, cool, trendy urban-types with a host of questions about God.

In the early years of our church I would meet with anyone who had questions about God because I am a pastor who deeply loves his people. But as our church grew, I simply became unable to meet with all the people who had questions and needed answers. So, I wrote the first version of this book (a small, self-published booklet) to give to the people whom I pastor at Mars Hill Church in Seattle. It was my hope that God would use the booklet to help people understand who God is so they could have a life-changing relationship of loving trust with him. Over the years, many thousands of copies of that booklet have been given away, which prompted my friends at Crossway to invite me to rewrite the material for this book in an effort to also serve you in love. This modest book is an attempt to briefly and simply explain who God is through the lens of both philosophy and theology. Certainly this book could be an entire library of books explaining in great detail the person and work of God, and this is therefore not intended to be exhaustive, but rather introductory in nature.

1

Knowledge about God

We live in an age of seemingly endless gods, goddesses, religions, and spiritualities. As a result, it is very difficult to pursue knowledge of God. After all, if there is such widespread disagreement over whether or not God or gods exist, why should anyone try to form his or her own conclusions on the matter? Moreover, if someone wanted to arrive at a personal conviction on the question of whether or not there is a God, how should he or she begin the journey? Historically, much ink has been spilled over this matter, and I will seek to briefly explain some of the common conclusions.

To begin, we must determine whether or not a God or gods and goddesses do actually exist. Many philosophical arguments have been proposed to prove the existence of God. Among the most popular are the arguments from the highest ideal (ontological argument), intelligent design (teleological argument), first cause (cosmological argument), time (Kalam argument), and morality (axiological argument). Each of these arguments is complex and can be presented in multiple ways. Generally speaking, these philosophical arguments are each inductive in form, meaning they reason from what God has done to an understanding of who God is. The one exception is the ontological argument, which is a deductive argument. To help you consider the merits of these arguments, I will summarize each briefly.

Ontological Argument from Highest Ideal

The philosopher Anselm of Canterbury (1033–1109) first formulated the argument from the highest ideal, also called the ontological argument (*ontos* means "being"). The ontological argument seeks to prove the existence of God by reasoning that human beings, regardless of their culture or period in history, continually conceive of a perfect being that is greater than they are—so great that no greater being can be conceived of. This perfect being is God. The argument follows that since the human mind is only able to conceive of that which actually exists, God must exist because we would not be able to conceive of God unless there was God. Likewise, everything else that we conceive of, from automobiles to the color blue, does exist. Therefore, our idea about this perfect highest being called God is derived from the actual existence of this God. This argument is rooted in Exodus 3:14, where God reveals himself to Moses as "I AM WHO I AM."

Historically, this argument for the existence of God has been highly controversial. Its defenders include René Descartes (1596–1650) and Benedict Spinoza (1632–1677). Its critics include Christian Thomas Aquinas (1225–1274) and atheist David Hume (1711–1776). While not without merit, this argument's complexity and controversy make it perhaps not the most compelling argument for God's existence in comparison to the inductive arguments that we will now explore.

Teleological Argument from Design

The teleological argument seeks to convince from the amazing harmony in all of creation that the world has been ordered by an Intelligent Designer who is God. The name itself bears this out, as it is taken from the word *telos*, which means purpose or design. In its simple form, the argument contends that when we see something that is designed, we rightly assume that it was created by an intelligent designer. Further, the more complicated something is, the more intelligent the designer must have been. For example, if we were walking through the woods and found a small house built out of Legos, we would not only assume that it was created by an intelligent designer, but we may also surmise that a child was responsible for the creation. On the other hand, if we found a fifty-story building complete with central heating and a solar-powered electrical system, we would assume that not only was the building created, but also that the designer was more intelligent than that of the Lego building, namely a skilled architect.

The teleological argument finds biblical support in regards to the universe in such places as Psalm 19:1: "The heavens declare the glory of God, and the sky above proclaims his handiwork" and Romans 1:20: "[God's] invisible attributes, namely, his eternal power and divine nature, have been clearly perceived, ever since the creation of the world, in the things that have been made."

Support for the argument in regards to our own bodies is found in Psalm 139:13–14, which says, "For you formed my inward parts; you knitted me together in my mother's womb. I praise you, for I am fearfully and wonderfully made. Wonderful are your works. . . ." Further findings in science continually increase our understanding of the wondrous complexity of our body, including the fact that just one human DNA molecule holds roughly the same amount of information as one volume of an encyclopedia.

God himself even used teleological reasoning in an argument with a man named Job. Beginning in Job 38:1, God peppers Job with sixty-four questions about the design of creation, including: "Where were you when I laid the foundation of the earth? Tell me, if you have understanding."[1] As an aside, God's questioning of Job was God seeking in love to bring Job to the understanding that just as God had a purposeful design for his creation, so too he had a purposeful design in mind for Job's suffering.

Advocates of the teleological argument from design include Christian philosopher Thomas Aquinas. Perhaps the most famous articulation of the argument was by William Paley (1743–1805). His watchmaker analogy stated that if you came across something as complex as a watch, you would rightly assume that an intelligent designer made it. Likewise, as we walk through the world, we continually encounter things made with far greater complexity than a watch, such as the eye you are using to read these words. Therefore, we are logically compelled to believe that these things were intelligently designed by God. Although belief in an Intelligent Designer became less prominent as a result of the rise of modern science, many scientists, including non-Christians, have accepted the intelligent design theory as quantum mechanics has replaced Newtonian physics as the prevailing scientific worldview. Furthermore, numerous media outlets including *Time* and *PBS* have featured stories on the growing acceptance of intelligent design theory in recent years.

In recent decades, the "fine-tuning argument" has also gained prominence as a form of the teleological argument. Astrophysicists, such as the Christian Hugh Ross, and others proposing the argument note that several basic physical constants must fall within very narrow limits if intelligent life is to develop. For example, our world's constant gravitational force, the rate of universe expansion, the average distance between stars, the nature of gravity, earth's distance from the sun, earth's rotation period,

1. Job 38:4.

and even our carbon dioxide levels are so finely tuned for life on our planet that no logical explanation other than God is tenable.

Cosmological Argument from First Cause

The cosmological argument comes from the word *cosmos*, which means "orderly arrangement." The word was purportedly first used to explain the universe by the sixth-century-BC Greek philosopher Pythagoras. The argument from first cause asserts that for every effect there is a cause. (This is referred to formally as the law of causality.) Therefore, the material world must have a beginning, and that beginning must be outside of the material world to cause it to come into existence. The first cause, also called the uncaused cause, is God. On this point, the astronomer Fred Hoyle claimed that "the probability of life arising on earth (by purely natural means, without special divine aid) is less than the probability that a flight-worthy Boeing 747 should be assembled by a hurricane roaring through a junkyard."[2]

This argument has been popular with many non-Christian thinkers such as Plato (428–348 BC), Aristotle (384–322 BC), the Muslim philosopher Al-Farabi (872–950), as well as the Jewish thinker Moses Maimonides (1135–1204). Noteworthy Christian thinkers advocating the cosmological argument include Augustine (354–430), Anselm, Descartes, and Aquinas. They have reasoned that in addition to the material world, immaterial things such as emotions and intelligence are simply not possible apart from a God who created the world in general and humans in particular. Simply, the cause of our emotions and thoughts cannot be emotionless and unintelligent matter.

2. Fred Hoyle, quoted in Alvin Plantinga, "The Dawkins Confusion," *Books & Culture* 13, no. 2 (March/April 2007): 21, http://www.christianitytoday.com/bc/2007/002/1.21.html.

Therefore, we must have been created by an emotional and intelligent God, which explains the effect of our feelings and thoughts.

The cosmological argument for creation from a first cause is rooted in many places in Scripture. The biblical creation story tells us that an eternal, necessary first cause (God) created the universe and all that is in it. God is eternal[3] and is therefore separate and apart from his creation as the necessary first cause. The first two chapters of Genesis report that God eternally existed before any aspect of creation and that God alone is the Creator and Cause of our world.

In explaining how God is the cause of creation, it is common to hear the phrase *ex nihilo*. *Ex nihilo* is Latin for "out of nothing" and is commonly used to explain how God made creation out of nothing. The Bible teaches that God made creation *ex nihilo* in Hebrews 11:3, which says, "By faith we understand that the universe was created by the word of God, so that what is seen was not made out of things that are visible."

Opponents of this argument have sought to negate its claims by offering alternatives to the concept that the world had a cause and a beginning. For example, solipsists suggest that the world is simply an illusion. Nevertheless, they hypocritically look both ways before crossing a busy street. Some have argued that the world is self-created, which seems as illogical as coming home to find a new flat-screen television complete with remote control and high-definition cable and believing that the television, remote, and cable hookup each caused itself to spring into existence and work together in perfect harmony. Others have reasoned that the material world came from nothing and was made by nothing, which also seems illogical because no-thing cannot create a-thing. Believing that matter and energy sprang from nothing requires a leap of faith more giant than believing that creation is the work of God. Finally, others

3. Ps. 90:2.

have opposed the argument from first cause by suggesting that the universe is eternal. Yet most scientists believe that the universe is winding down to an eventual end based upon the Second Law of Thermodynamics and the Big Bang Theory, which proves that it likewise had a beginning. This leads us to the argument from time, which we will examine next. As a curious historical footnote, even the great father of evolution, Charles Darwin, was clear in *On the Origin of Species* that he remained convinced that God existed in agreement with the cosmological argument.

Kalam Argument from Time

The basic Kalam argument is that the existence of time necessitates a beginning as a reference point from which time proceeds. This reference point would have to be outside of time to begin time, and that eternal reference point is God, who is outside of time but initiated time. To put it another way, the universe is not eternal and therefore must have a beginning. Behind that beginning must be a cause that is eternal, or apart from time. Therefore, the cause of time and creation is God.

This argument relies heavily on the Second Law of Thermodynamics, which affirms that the universe is running out of usable energy and is therefore winding down to an end. Practically, this means that since the universe will have an end, it is not eternal and must have also had a beginning. Also used in support of this argument is Big Bang cosmology, which states that the universe had a beginning and has been expanding ever since and is therefore not eternal.

The argument from time was formulated by Muslim philosophers such as Al-Farabi and Al-Ghazali (1058–1111) and is now popular among Muslims, Jews, Protestants, and Catholics who teach that the existence of time is evidence for God.

The argument does have merits and is helpful, but it does not prove that God is personal or intelligent. Neither does it determine the nature of God as deistic, pantheistic, or monotheistic. Therefore, by itself the Kalam argument can help us believe in a god but cannot clearly articulate any specific information about the nature of God.

Axiological Argument from Morality

The axiological argument takes its title from the word *axios*, which means "judgment." The argument from morality contends that everyone, regardless of his or her culture, has an innate understanding of right and wrong. Simply, all sane people know that such things as rape and murder are wrong.

But where do these universal morals that exist in each of us come from? The moral argument responds that God has made us with a conscience that helps us navigate through life as responsible moral beings, though we often ignore the conscience he has given us. When we argue that the way something is is not the way it "ought" to be, the moral argument proponents would say we are not merely appealing to law, but ultimately to God who is the giver of the moral law implanted in our consciences.

This argument does agree with Scripture, which repeatedly appeals to our conscience in the knowledge of what is right and wrong. One such example is found in Romans 2:15, which speaks of non-Christians who are aware of their consciences: "the work of the law is written on their hearts, while their conscience also bears witness, and their conflicting thoughts accuse or even excuse them." Simply, when we feel bad about what we have done or what someone else has done, we are bearing witness that God is the Lawgiver and has put an understanding of his law on our hearts through our conscience.

The axiological argument was formalized by the philosopher Immanuel Kant (1724–1804) and winsomely articulated by the great Christian thinker C. S. Lewis (1898–1963). Lewis insightfully commented that when we have been sinned against, we often appeal to the universal laws that define right and wrong, assuming that there is an authority above the person who acted unjustly toward us. We also anticipate that somehow everyone else will agree with our understanding of right and wrong because we know that they have a conscience in them, which explains why we appeal to it.

One of the beautiful results of the moral law is that it permits us to have a righteous anger. Because there is both a Lawgiver and Law, we are able to rise above the incessant postmodern pluralism that says that there is no Law but only cultural perspective on morality. Because the axiological argument is true, we do not have to accept evil atrocities and injustices committed in one culture; instead, as human beings we can appeal to the higher authority of God the Lawgiver who sits over all cultures in authority. This explains, for example, why Nazi Germany was stopped for violating God's unchanging laws regarding human dignity and not merely accepted as a law unto itself. Curiously, at the Nuremberg trials, one of the more common appeals by those on trial was that there was no Lawgiver or Law, and that they were simply obeying the law of their nation. In response, the axiological argument was given because human beings were made with a sense of right and wrong by a moral God who is our Lawgiver. Other glorious examples of the practical outworking of the axiological law are Abraham Lincoln's (1809–1865) and William Wilberforce's (1759–1833) battles against slavery, as well as Martin Luther King Jr.'s (1929–1968) fight for civil rights from religious convictions.

In conclusion, taken together as a cumulative case, the various arguments for God's existence reveal that God exists; he is the Intelligent Designer, the powerful Cause of all creation, apart from time but at work in time, and morally good.

Pascal's Wager

After surveying the varying arguments for the existence of God, you may remain unconvinced that God exists. To help convince you to continually pursue the truth about God, it will be helpful to examine the thoughts of Blaise Pascal (1623–1662). At the age of fourteen, Pascal was invited to join a weekly gathering of the leading geometricians from Paris. By the age of sixteen, he had written a groundbreaking book on geometry that some critics rejected, believing it was far too complicated to have been conceived by someone of his young age. At the age of nineteen, Pascal invented the first calculator in an effort to assist his father with complex mathematics. He made some fifty such machines, which became the distant cousins of the modern-day computer.

At the age of thirty-one, Pascal invented probability theory in response to questions his friend posed to him regarding gambling. He also clarified theories on pressure and vacuum, studied hydraulic fluids, created the first hydraulic press, and invented the syringe. Additionally, he created the first public transportation system, which was a bus line built for the poor residents of Paris. His scientific legacy is so profound that today an SI unit of pressure as well as a computer program are named in honor of Pascal.

Tragically, Pascal, who was sick throughout his life, died in Paris on August 19, 1662, two months after his thirty-ninth birthday. He never did get to write his crowning book; *Pensées* ("Thoughts") is simply a compilation of the various thoughts he had scattered on scraps of paper. Amazingly, his unfinished thoughts alone were so profound that they remain a bestselling book over three hundred years later.

With his death imminent, Blaise Pascal gave his home to a poor family suffering with smallpox. Fittingly, Pascal's final words from his deathbed were, "May God never abandon me."

Pascal's now-famous concept of "The Wager" is described in *Pensées*:

> "Either God is or he is not." But to which view shall we be inclined? Reason cannot decide this question. Infinite chaos separates us. At the far end of this infinite distance a coin is being spun which will come down heads or tails. How will you wager? Reason cannot make you choose either, reason cannot prove either wrong. . . . Yes, but you must wager. There is no choice, you are already committed. . . . Let us weigh up the gain and the loss involved in calling heads that God exists. Let us assess the two cases: if you win you win everything, if you lose you lose nothing. Do not hesitate then; wager that he does exist.[4]

The gist of Pascal's argument is that life is a voyage toward or away from God that we embarked on the moment we were born. When it comes to believing in God, everything begins with a bet that everyone makes with his or her life. If you believe there is a God and you die to discover you are right, then you win your bet. If you believe in God and then die, but there is no God, you have lost nothing, gained nothing, and simply come out even on your bet. This bet is safe because you have nothing to lose and everything to gain.

On the other hand, if you do not believe in God, you are making a very risky bet, because you have everything to lose and nothing to gain. If you do not believe in

4. Blaise Pascal, *Pensées*, trans. A. J. Krailsheimer (New York: Penguin, 1966), 150–51.

God and when you die you discover you were wrong, you literally have hell to pay. And if you do not believe in God and then die and God does not exist, then you have gained nothing, lost nothing, and simply come out even on your bet. Pascal's point is that your life is a bet, and it is most reasonable to bet that there is a God.

Clearly, Pascal's wager is limited: Pascal does not tell us which God or gods we should worship. Most religions teach that their God is the only God. As a result, even if you do bet on a god, you will still end up in some form of hell if you've bet on the wrong God, gods, or goddesses. Therefore, even though Pascal's wager wisely encourages us to start pursuing God, we must go further. The question persists: how can we know God?

In his defense, Pascal's intentions with "The Wager" were modest. Rather than trying to answer every question someone may have about God, he merely sought to motivate people to pursue true knowledge of God. Indeed, he may have been guided by sections of Scripture such as Jeremiah 29:13–14a, where God says, "You will seek me and find me. When you seek me with all your heart. I will be found by you." In light of this, Pascal was not trying to convince people about God as much as compel them to pursue the truth for themselves.

The pursuit of that truth about God is likely the very reason why you are reading this book in the first place. To arrive at the truth about God, we must move from philosophical speculation, which is the human attempt to discover God, to biblical revelation, which is God's attempt to reveal himself to us. This move is vital because God, who is infinite, cannot be uncovered by those of us who are part of his finite creation unless he reveals himself to us.

Fortunately, the Bible has a lot to say about God revealing himself to us. The Bible repeatedly teaches that the truth about God can be truly known.[5] At the same time,

5. Jer. 9:24; John 17:3; 2 Tim. 1:12.

the Bible teaches that God cannot be fully known because he is infinite. We are finite and, therefore, incapable of understanding all that he is and does.[6] The Bible further describes some of the reasons we are unable to fully know God: (1) he has secrets that he will not reveal to us;[7] (2) as a result of our finitude and sin, we see only in part;[8] (3) he hides parts of his person from our knowledge;[9] and (4) we suppress much of what God has made known to us about himself because we don't like what God says.[10] Thus, arriving at a true knowledge of God requires both a desire to learn what has been revealed and a humility to follow the truth wherever it should lead us. In that spirit, we start our journey to the truth about God by first wandering down some of the philosophical and religious paths that do not lead to God.

6. Job 11:7–8; Pss. 97:2; 145:3; Isa. 40:28; 45:15; 55:8–9; 1 Cor. 2:11.
7. Deut. 29:29.
8. 1 Cor. 13:12.
9. Isa. 45:15.
10. Rom. 1:18–25.

Perspectives about God

Theology literally means the "study of God," and to follow the path of truth to God we must first determine which path that is. The difficulty is that varying religions and philosophies have divergent proposed understandings of what the truth is about God. In an effort to help you understand many of the most prominent perspectives on God, we will now explore the various paths that meander through the complicated world of *isms*.

Atheism comes from the negative *a-*, which means "no," "not," or "without," and *theos*, which means "god." Basically, atheism is the belief that there is no God. Related to atheism are the beliefs that there is no devil, no supernatural realm, no miracles, no absolute moral truth, and nothing beyond the material world, so therefore people do not have souls and there is no possibility of spiritual life after physical death.

Curiously, atheism is a relatively new concept. The word *atheism* does not exist in the Hebrew language, in which the Old Testament was written. Moreover, the Old Testament assumes that everyone believes in the existence of God. This explains why the Old Testament speaks of atheists rather mockingly by saying, "The fool says in his heart, 'There is no God.'"[1]

1. Pss. 14:1; 53:1.

Chart 2.1 *Perspectives on God*

Theory/Doctrine	Belief
Atheism	There is no God.
Agnosticism	God cannot be known.
Deism	God is not active in the world.
Finite Godism	God is limited.
Pantheism	God is the world.
Panentheism	All is in God.
Polytheism	There are many gods/goddesses.
Monotheism	There is one God.
Trinitarianism	There is one God in three persons.

In the past, atheism was purported by the communist Karl Marx (1818–1883), capitalist Ayn Rand (1905–1982), psychologist Sigmund Freud (1856–1939), and philosopher Friedrich Nietzsche (1844–1900). Atheism also occasionally makes a comeback. In more recent years, it has rebounded as a hip worldview featured on magazine covers such as *Wired*. The new pope of atheism is one of the world's most popular science writers, Richard Dawkins. His book *The God Delusion* is a polemically toned philosophical rebuttal to the possibility of God's existence. Alvin Plantinga, professor of philosophy at the University of Notre Dame, writes of Dawkins's book: "Dawkins is not a philosopher (he's a biologist). Even taking this into account, however, much of the philosophy he purveys is at best jejune. You might say that some of his forays into philosophy are at best sophomoric, but that would be unfair to sophomores; the fact is (grade inflation aside), many of his arguments would receive a failing grade in a sophomore philosophy class. This, combined with the arrogant, smarter-than-thou tone of the book, can be annoying."[2]

For those wanting to read further responses to Dawkins's book, the appendixes to this book list some recommended resources. For the sake of brevity, I will simply say that in the end, atheism suffers under the burden of proof. For example, Jesus himself claimed to be God, which is in stark conflict with the entire premise of atheism, a point we will examine more fully in chapter 5. Further, in stating that there is no god, atheism must prove that God does not exist; this requires that we have complete knowledge, which is impossible. Consequently, agnosticism has become more popular among those who doubt the existence of a God or gods.

Agnosticism is derived from *a-*, meaning "without," and *Gnosticism* or *gnosis*, meaning "knowledge." An agnostic does not know about or is ignorant about God. Some of the more famous agnostic philosophers include Thomas Henry Huxley (1825–1895) and Bertrand Russell (1872–1970).

Agnosticism asserts that while we can examine the physical world, we have no access to the spiritual world and therefore can never know if a God or gods exists. The agnostic position overlooks the possibility that if God exists, he could reveal himself to us and thereby make himself known. This is precisely what the Bible teaches about Jesus. The Bible says that Jesus "descended from heaven."[3] John also describes Jesus in this way: "And the Word became flesh and dwelt among us, and we have seen his glory, glory as of the only Son from the Father, full of grace and truth."[4] Furthermore,

2. Alvin Plantinga, "The Dawkins Confusion," *Books & Culture* 13, no. 2 (March/April 2007): 21, http://www.christianitytoday.com/bc/2007/002/1.21.html.

3. John 3:13; 6:38.

4. John 1:14.

Jesus himself says, "Whoever has seen me has seen the Father."[5] Therefore, agnosticism is an untenable position because Jesus came down from heaven and revealed God to us in order to overcome our spiritual ignorance. Jesus clears the fog of agnosticism so that we can see God clearly.

Deism teaches that a god did in fact make the universe but then left his creation alone and has no dealings with it. The deist god is a sort of absentee landlord. With god no longer involved in his creation, deism teaches that the world runs by natural laws that god established to govern his creation. Subsequently, miracles are impossible because the universe is a closed system, and god does not intervene in his creation or overrule his natural laws. Although the popularity of deism has waned in recent generations (with the exception of Unitarians and spiritual humanists who also deny the Trinity and hell), there was a day when it was popular with the likes of Thomas Hobbes (1588–1679), Ben Franklin (1706–1790), and Thomas Paine (1737–1809).

Perhaps the most noted and consistent deist was President Thomas Jefferson (1743–1826). He once sat down in the White House with a razor in one hand and the Bible in the other and cut out those parts of Scripture that he decided were untrue. The result was *The Philosophy of Jesus of Nazareth*, or *The Life and Morals of Jesus of Nazareth*. Only one in ten verses survived, zero miracles were considered factual, and the resurrection of Jesus was systematically cut from the pages of Scripture.

The inconsistencies with deism are many, including the fact that they deny miracles yet affirm the great miracle of creation by God. In addition, the new theories in science such as quantum physics have all but overruled the older concepts of Newtonian physics, upon which deism rested for its legitimization. Furthermore, the Scriptures

5. John 14:9.

teach that Jesus is not only the Creator God of the universe, but also the ongoing Sustainer God who contradicts the central tenet of deism: "For by him [Jesus] all things were created, in heaven and on earth, visible and invisible, whether thrones or dominions or rulers or authorities—all things were created through him and for him. And he is before all things, and in him all things hold together."[6]

Finite Godism postulates that god does exist but with limitations, such as not being all knowing (omniscient) or all powerful (omnipotent). The motivation behind finite godism is to explain how a good god could coexist with all of the evil and injustice in the world. Finite godism seeks to explain the goodness of god and the evil in the world by stating that while god is good, god is incapable and simply cannot do anything to stop the evil in the world. While no major religion holds to finite godism, it has street cred with many ordinary people who believe in god and assume his hands are tied in the world, much like ours are.

The problems with finite godism are many. First, a finite god would need a greater infinite God to enable its continued existence. Second, past and present evil does not negate the fact that the all-powerful, infinite God will one day bring evil to an end, as Scripture teaches. Third, the existence of evil does not in any way disprove the infinite wisdom and power of God. Fourth, a finite god is simply of no help at all; such a flaccidly impotent god cannot truly help us in our time of need and is therefore unworthy of worship or prayer.

However, Jesus answers the question motivating the belief in finite godism. At the cross of Jesus we witness the darkest hour of humanity. At the hands of an unjust legal system, surrounded by chants of a mob thirsty for blood, the greatest person

6. Col. 1:16–17.

who has ever lived, Jesus Christ, was brutally murdered. In that moment, it appeared that God was in fact finite as he did nothing to intervene and stop the injustice. Yet, three days later Jesus rose from the grave. God demonstrated himself not as powerless but powerful. Through the cross, the most glorious victory ever has been won; our sin was forgiven through Jesus' suffering and painful death. Therefore, through the life, death, and resurrection of Jesus, the question, where is God when it hurts? (which plagues the adherents of finite godism) is answered: God is good and powerful and at work to bring about victory and life, even through what appears at first glance to be nothing more than defeat and death.

Pantheism is derived from *pan*, which means "all" and *theism*, which means "god." Pantheism is thus the belief that all is god or, in other words, that the material world is itself god or divine. Based upon monism, which is the belief that all reality is one being, the result is that the god of pantheism is impersonal. Pantheism is most popular in religions such as Hinduism and some forms of Buddhism along with New Spirituality (also called New Age-ism), Christian Science, Unity Church, Scientology, and Theosophy. Pantheism was most widely advocated in the worldview of *Star Wars,* where God is not a person but rather a kind of force that envelopes and includes each of us.

In pantheism there are no miracles because God is not beyond this world or able to override it. It is also said that pain, matter, and evil are unreal illusions, which does not make any sense after you stub your toe as you leave your yoga class.

Pantheism has many other shortcomings, including denying that the universe had a beginning when both Big Bang cosmology and the Second Law of Thermodynamics declare otherwise, declaring the physical world to be an illusion, and an inability to explain how a world without intelligence or morality brought both into existence. Pantheism is clearly refuted in Romans 1:25: "They [people who do not know God] exchanged the truth about God for a lie and worshiped and served the creature rather than the Creator, who is blessed forever! Amen." In this verse, Paul articulates that it is wise to worship the Creator and foolish to worship his creation, as pantheism encourages.

Panentheism comes from *pan* ("all") + *in* + *theism* ("god"), which together mean "all in God." Not to be confused with pantheism, panentheism teaches that God is part of or in creation so that, in a way, creation is akin to God's body. In panentheism, God is seen as existing in two polarities; God exists in one form as a present reality and exists in another form as a future possibility. It is said that God is growing, maturing, and evolving from his current state to his potential state. As a result, it is said that God is both finite and infinite, and eternal without a beginning yet not eternal and with a beginning. Contradicting itself, panentheism therefore teaches that God made himself, which would require God to exist before he existed. Furthermore, panentheism says that God is presently imperfect but ever learning, growing, and changing to become more and more perfect.

The self-contradictions of panentheism are readily apparent, yet this belief was held in the ancient world by men such as Plato and in more recent times by the influential philosophers G. W. F. Hegel (1770–1831) and Alfred North Whitehead (1861–1947). Tragically, some who profess to be Christian have also adopted the false understanding of God postulated by panentheism. This includes some feminist theologians, Marxist theologians, the emerging church leader Spencer Burke, and even the former president of what is supposed to be an evangelical seminary near our church, who simply announced to his class, which included one of our pastors, that he was a panentheist. A panentheistic view of God also shows up in such things as process theology and some forms of what is called open theism, both of which stress the immanence of God over his transcendence and the changing of God over his immutability.

Panentheism does not agree with the God of the Bible. Some of God's attributes, which we will examine in the next chapter, include his immutability, his perfection, his sovereignty (he is not bound in creation), his infiniteness, and his independence of the world rather than dependence upon it. Simply, God is not like a moody junior high kid with a lot of potential that he is hoping to fulfill once he grows out of deity puberty.

Polytheism comes from *poly*, which means "many," and *theism*, which means "god." Polytheism teaches that there is more than one god. Religions adhering to polytheism include Hinduism, Confucianism, Shintoism, Taoism, Jainism, ancient Greek mythology, Mormonism, Scientology, and the Unification Church.

The main problem with polytheism is that it is impossible for multiple, completely equal, finite gods to exist without a superior and infinite God to rule as their Creator and overseer. Clearly, the Bible acknowledges that many people worship false gods. There is only one true God[7] and all other "gods" are mere idols and not "gods" at all.[8] However, demons (fallen angels) may also pose as gods and elicit worship, possibly even through counterfeit signs, wonders, and miracles.[9] The Old Testament is clear that there is only one God.[10] The New Testament agrees that there is only one

7. 2 Chron. 15:3; Jer. 10:10; John 17:3; 1 Thess. 1:9; 1 John 5:20–21.
8. Deut. 32:21; 1 Sam. 12:21; Ps. 96:5; Isa. 37:19; 41:23–24, 29; Jer. 2:11; 5:7; 16:20; 1 Cor. 8:4; 10:19–20.
9. Deut. 32:17; Ps. 106:37; 1 Cor. 10:18–22; Gal. 4:8.
10. Deut. 4:35, 39; 6:4–5; 32:39; 1 Sam. 2:2; 2 Sam. 7:22; 22:32; Ps. 86:8–10; Isa. 37:20; 43:10; 44:6–8; 45:5, 14, 21–22; 46:9.

God.[11] The Bible also teaches that there is no one like God.[12] Thus, claiming to be like God is a satanic lie.[13] Therefore, polytheism is abhorred throughout Scripture as errant at best and evil at worst.

Monotheism teaches that there is only one personal God who is separate (transcendent) from the universe though involved in it (immanent). As a result, many people have regarded Christianity as just one of many monotheistic religions along with Judaism and Islam. In one sense, Christianity is monotheistic, as it does believe in one God. Yet, upon further investigation, the Bible is not impressed with mere monotheism because God's objective is not that we simply believe in one God. As James 2:19 says, "You believe that God is one; you do well. Even the demons believe—and shudder!"

The God of Christianity as revealed in the Bible is one God who exists in the Trinitarian community of Father, Son, and Spirit, which we will now examine as the one true God.

Trinitarianism is the Christian teaching that there is one God who exists as three persons: Father, Son, and Spirit. While the word *trinity* does not appear in Scripture, the concept very clearly does. The church father Tertullian (AD 155–220) was the first to use the word *trinity*. To say that God exists as a trinity does not mean there are three Gods, or that one God merely manifests himself as either Father, Son, or

11. John 5:44; Rom. 3:30; 16:27; 1 Cor. 8:4–6; Gal. 3:20; Eph. 4:6; 1 Tim. 1:17; 2:5; James 2:19; Jude 25.

12. Ex. 8:10; 9:14; 15:11; 2 Sam. 7:22; 1 Kings 8:23; 1 Chron. 17:20; Ps. 86:8; Isa. 40:18, 25; 44:7; 46:5, 9; Jer. 10:6–7; Mic. 7:18.

13. Gen. 3:5; Isa. 14:14; John 8:44.

Holy Spirit on various occasions. Rather, it means that there is one God with a unified essence who exists in three equal persons: Father, Son, and Holy Spirit. By person it is meant that God thinks, feels, acts, and speaks. The Westminster Confession of Faith (1647) summarizes the doctrine by saying, "In the unity of the Godhead there be three persons, of one substance, power, and eternity: God the Father, God the Son, and God the Holy Ghost."[14]

In addition to believing that there is only one God,[15] Trinitarianism also recognizes the biblical teaching that the Father, Son, and Spirit are each eternally God. Throughout the Scriptures, the Father is unequivocally called God.[16] Jesus Christ is clearly called God throughout the Scriptures.[17] The Holy Spirit is also declared to be God.[18] In addition, God the Holy Spirit is not merely an impersonal force, but a person who can be grieved,[19] resisted,[20] and insulted.[21]

Additionally, though the Father, Son, and Spirit are one, the Father and Son are referred to as two distinct persons in frequent salutations of New Testament letters,[22] as well as in other Scriptures.[23] The Scriptures are also clear that Jesus and

14. Westminster Confession of Faith, 2.3.

15. Deut. 6:4–5; 1 Tim. 2:5.

16. John 6:27; 17:1, 3; 1 Cor. 8:6; 2 Cor. 1:3; Eph. 1:3; 1 Pet. 1:3.

17. Matt. 28:9; John 1:1–4, 14; 5:17–18; 8:58; 10:30–33; 12:37–41, cf. Isa. 6:9–11; John 20:28–29; Acts 20:28; Rom. 9:5; Col. 1:16–17; 2:8–9; Phil. 2:10–11; Heb. 1:8; 1 Cor. 8:4–6; 1 Tim. 6:15; Titus 2:13; 1 John 5:20; Rev. 1:8, 17–18; 17:14; 19:16; 22:13–16.

18. John 14:16; Acts 5:3–4; 2 Cor. 3:16–18.

19. Eph. 4:30.

20. Acts 7:51.

21. Heb. 10:29.

22. Rom. 1:7; 1 Cor. 1:3; 2 Cor. 1:2; Gal. 1:3; Eph. 1:2; 6:23; Phil. 1:2; 1 Thess. 1:1; 2 Thess. 1:12; 1 Tim. 1:1–2; 2 Tim. 1:2; Titus 1:4; Philem. 3; James 1:1; 2 Pet. 1:2; 2 John 3.

23. John 3:17; 5:31–32; 8:16–18; 11:41–42; 12:28; 14:31; 17:23–26; Gal. 4:4; 1 John 4:10.

the Holy Spirit are not the same person.[24] Likewise, the Father is not the Holy Spirit.[25]

The following Scriptures provide helpful insight on the Trinity. Each verse speaks of the Father, Son, and Spirit together as the One God:

- "And when Jesus was baptized, immediately he went up from the water, and behold, the heavens were opened to him, and he saw the Spirit of God descending like a dove and coming to rest on him; and behold, a voice from heaven [the Father] said, 'This is my beloved Son, with whom I am well pleased.'"[26]

- "And Jesus came and said to them, 'All authority in heaven and on earth has been given to me. Go therefore and make disciples of all nations, baptizing them in the name of the Father and of the Son and of the Holy Spirit, teaching them to observe all that I have commanded you. And behold, I am with you always, to the end of the age.'"[27]

The concept of the Trinity reveals that the God of the Bible is in himself relational. Some religions teach that God made people to cure his loneliness; conversely, the fact is that God as a Trinitarian community was never without loving community. Rather, he is a relational God who welcomes us into relationship with himself.

Clearly, the Christian belief in the Trinitarian God of Scripture is unique. This is in part because while the unaided human mind could conceive of a world without

24. Luke 3:22; John 14:16; 15:26; 16:7.
25. John 14:15–17; 15:26; Rom. 8:11, 26–27; 2 Cor. 1:3–4.
26. Matt. 3:16–17.
27. Matt. 28:18–20.

God (atheism), have uncertainty about God (agnosticism), perceive God as absent (deism), misunderstand God as impotent (finite godism), worship creation as God (pantheism), limit God in creation (panentheism), embrace multiple gods/goddesses (polytheism), or conclude there must be one supreme god (monotheism), only God through revelation could inform us of the complicated understanding of one God who eternally exists as three persons who love and communicate perfectly and are the source of all life and love. As a result of this unique understanding of God, Christianity is distinct from all other religions, philosophies, and spiritualities and therefore not merely another religion or philosophy with a perspective of God, but rather the truth of who God has revealed himself to be.

In closing, I pray that this chapter will help you to see the incredibly significant differences between various perspectives about God that cannot each be true. In our age it is not uncommon for people to say that all religions are the same, as if the major world religions (Buddhism, Christianity, Confucianism, Hinduism, Islam, Jainism, Judaism, Shintoism, Sikhism, Taoism, and Zoroastrianism), along with the countless minor religions, all have the same view of God. Meanwhile, their views of God consist of one God, many gods, all is God, God is in all, there is no God, God as personal and impersonal, immanent and transcendent, finite and infinite, and, in some cases, a contradictory "all of the above." To make matters worse, various religions define the human problem differently, as sin, ignorance, or a lack of enlightenment, with salvation being offered through Jesus' grace, our religious devotion, or meditation and reincarnation.

Simply put, not all religions and their perspectives about God are the same, despite the popular notion otherwise. One of the more popularized arguments for the acceptance of all the perspectives we have studied is the elephant analogy. This is the story of numerous blind men who arrive upon an elephant. Upon touching a leg, one man thinks it is a tree; upon touching the trunk, another man thinks it is a snake; and upon touching a tusk, yet another blind man thinks it is a spear. The moral of the story, we are told, is that each man is embracing the same reality with simply a different perspective and that the same is true of how various religions see God. In response, it deserves noting that God opens our spiritual eyes so that we are not blind. At the end of the day, the animal from the story was still an elephant (not a tree or a snake or a spear), because the truth is the truth; it is the same with God as it is with the elephant. We will now proceed to learn more about the true God through the revelation of his attributes in Scripture.

3

Nature of God

According to Christian Scripture, God is not an idea, but instead a living and free person who is completely different, other, or "holy." Speaking about this entirely other God is difficult, so Christians often speak about God's attributes. These attributes are revealed to us in two ways: through Scripture and through our ongoing relationship with God through Jesus.

We know God through our experiences of relationship with him: when we recognize his presence all around us; when we recognize his provision in our lives; when we confess our sins and accept his grace to live by faith. By his loving friendship, we come to a fuller realization of who he truly is as revealed in Scripture.

God's attributes are inseparable from his very being. In every way that God exists, he exists without limit and in perfection. God's attributes can be divided into two categories: unshared and shared (also called incommunicable and communicable). His unshared attributes belong only to him, while his shared attributes are found in people to a limited degree, since we are created in his image and likeness. We will save his shared attributes for later in this chapter and begin our study of God's nature by examining his unshared attributes.

Unshared Attributes

Omniscience

God has perfect knowledge of all things, including the past, present, future, and everything actual or potential.[1] It is comforting to know that God knows all about us, yet still loves and forgives us. Since God knows everything, nothing can separate us from him, nothing can surprise him, and he knows all our needs.

Omnipotence

God is all powerful and able to do all that he wills.[2] It is God's power that guarantees assurance of our salvation.[3] Because of God's power over all else, we can trust God to work out our seemingly impossible situations for his glory and our good.[4]

Immutability

God does not change.[5] God is perfect and remains the same even when we change, and we can trust what God has said in Scripture because his Word never changes either.

Eternality

God has no beginning and no end and is not bound by time, although he created time, is conscious of time, and does work in time.[6] Because God sees things from an

1. Job 42:2; Pss. 139:1–6; 147:5; Isa. 40:12–14; 46:10; Heb. 4:13.
2. Job 42:2; Ps. 147:5; Matt. 19:26; Eph. 3:20.
3. Rom. 1:16; 8:35–39.
4. Gen. 18:14; Jer. 32:17, 27; Luke 1:37; Rom. 8:28.
5. Num. 23:19; Ps. 102:27; Mal. 3:6; Rom. 11:29; Heb. 13:8; James 1:17.
6. Pss. 90:2; 93:2; 102:12; Eph. 3:21.

eternal perspective, he knows what is best for our lives and for the events that take place in the world.

Self-Existence

God is the only being who is not controlled by external forces and does not depend upon anyone or anything for his continued existence.[7] It is reassuring to know God is the Creator of all things and all things are dependent upon him. Also, since God created us, he can sustain us and control our future for good.

Sovereignty

God is supreme in rule and authority over all things,[8] though he does allow human freedom as he wills.[9] No attribute can supply the security and comfort in terrible trials like God's sovereignty, because within our trials is the reminder that there is a God who is working out all things for our eventual good.[10]

Transcendence

God is fully distinct from the universe he created.[11] It is awe-inspiring and comforting to know the enormity and otherness of God and his infinite grandeur.

7. Ex. 3:14; Isa. 41:4; 43:10; 44:6; 48:12; Rev. 1:8, 17; 2:8; 3:14; 21:6; 22:13.
8. 2 Sam. 7:28; 1 Chron. 29:10–13; Ps. 103:19.
9. Gen. 50:20; Rom. 1:18–32.
10. Gen. 50:20; Rom. 8:28.
11. Gen. 1:1; Ps. 102:25–27; Isa. 42:5; Acts 17:24; 1 John 2:15–17.

Creator

God brought all things into existence out of nothing, solely by his power.[12] It is a pleasure to enjoy God's creation, and also amazing to consider he created all that is out of nothing by the sheer power of himself.

Names of God

In addition to God's attributes, we learn a great deal about God through the various names that are used to communicate aspects of his person. Therefore, we will now examine various names of God that are revealed to us in Scripture.

In Scripture, a person's name is closely linked to the person's character and purpose. This is also true of the names of God in Scripture. All names of God reveal something about God and his character.

Primary Old Testament Names

- *Yahweh* or *Jehovah* means "Self-Existent One" (such as when God called himself "I AM"[13]). The characteristics of this name have to do with the relationship between the true God and his people and, when used, emphasize God's holiness, hatred of sin, and love of sinners.
- *Elohim* means "Strong One."[14] This name reveals the true God who is more powerful than the false gods. It is often used in reference to God's sovereignty and work.[15]

12. Gen. 1:1; Pss. 33:6; 102:25; Isa. 44:24; John 1:3; Rom. 11:36; Heb. 1:2; 11:3.
13. Ex. 3:14.
14. Gen. 1:1.
15. Deut. 5:23; 8:11–15; Ps. 68:7; Isa. 45:18; 54:5; Jer. 32:27.

- *Adonai*, which means "Lord or Master," marks God out as the ruler over all people, times, places, and things.[16]

Compound Old Testament Names

With *El*

- *El Elyon*: the Most High, exalted one, or the strongest strong one.[17]
- *El Roi*: the Strong One who sees everything.[18]
- *El Shaddai*: the Almighty God, which points to his gracious power.[19]
- *El Olam*: the Everlasting God, the unchanging God.[20]

With *Jehovah*

- *Jehovah Jirah*: the Lord will provide.[21]
- *Jehovah Nissi*: the Lord my banner.[22]
- *Jehovah Shalom*: the Lord my peace.[23]
- *Jehovah Sabbaoth*: the Lord of hosts/angels.[24]
- *Jehovah Maccaddeshcem*: the Lord your Sanctifier.[25]
- *Jehovah Raah*: the Lord my Shepherd.[26]

16. Josh. 5:14; Isa. 6:8–11.
17. Gen. 14:19; Ps. 9:2; Isa. 14:13–14; Dan. 7:18, 22, 25.
18. Gen. 16:13.
19. Gen. 17:1–20; 28:3; 35:11; Ps. 91:1–2.
20. Gen. 16:13; Isa. 40:28.
21. Gen. 22:13–14.
22. Ex. 17:15.
23. Judg. 6:24.
24. 1 Sam. 1:3.
25. Ex. 31:13.
26. Ps. 23:1.

- *Jehovah Tsidkenu*: the Lord our righteousness.[27]
- *Jehovah El Gmolah*: the Lord God of recompense.[28]
- *Jehovah Nakeh*: the Lord who smites.[29]
- *Jehovah Shammah*: the Lord who is present.[30]

Names of God in the New Testament

When looking at the names of God in the New Testament, Jesus Christ emerges as the predominant name. The name *Jesus* is derived from the Hebrew Old Testament word *Joshua*, *Y'shua*, or *Je-Hoshua*, which means "Jehovah is Salvation." Jesus also referred to himself by the most sacred Old Testament name for God, "I am."[31] Through-out the Gospel of John, Jesus proclaimed, "I am the light of the world," "I am the bread of life," "I am living water," "I am the resurrection and the life," and "I am the way, and the truth, and the life." The name *Christ* also appears throughout the New Testament and is the equivalent to the Old Testament Hebrew *Messiah* (*Meshiach*), which means "the Anointed One." Therefore, the most common name for God in the New Testament is Jesus Christ.

Images of God

In addition to speaking of God in terms of his attributes and names, the Bible also speaks of God in poetic images intended to provoke our imagination to more fully comprehend who he is. Two types of poetic images describe God: those

27. Jer. 23:6.
28. Jer. 51:56.
29. Ezek. 7:9.
30. Ezek. 48:35.
31. John 8:58.

taken from human experience (anthropomorphic) and experiences taken from creation.

Anthropomorphic Poetic Images of God

- Bridegroom[32]
- Husband[33]
- Father[34]
- Judge[35]
- Warrior[36]
- Designer and Builder[37]
- Shepherd[38]
- King[39]
- Singer[40]
- Potter[41]
- Farmer[42]

32. Isa. 61:10.
33. Isa. 54:5.
34. Deut. 32:6.
35. Gen. 18:25.
36. Ex. 15:3.
37. Heb. 11:10.
38. Ps. 23:1.
39. Ex. 15:18.
40. Zeph. 3:17.
41. Jeremiah 18–19.
42. Isaiah 5.

- Refiner[43]
- Knitter[44]

Additionally, God is metaphorically described as walking[45] and smelling,[46] and having body parts such as hands,[47] a mouth,[48] eyes,[49] ears,[50] and a face.[51] This does not mean that God is a man; the Bible clearly states that "God is not man."[52] Yet God does reveal himself to us in terms that we can understand. Likewise, when God refers to himself as gathering his people under his wings like a hen,[53] it does not mean that God could be turned into a large plate of hot wings needing to be washed down with a beer, but rather that he appreciates the value of metaphor.

Poetic Images of God from Creation

God is compared to:

- A lion[54]
- An eagle[55]

43. Ps. 12:6.
44. Ps. 139:13.
45. Gen. 3:8.
46. Gen. 8:21.
47. Num. 11:23; Ps. 111:7.
48. Deut. 8:3.
49. Deut. 11:12.
50. 1 Pet. 3:12.
51. 1 Pet. 3:12.
52. Num. 23:19.
53. Matt. 23:37; Luke 13:34.
54. Isa. 31:4.
55. Deut. 32:11.

- A lamb[56]
- A hen[57]
- The sun[58]
- The morning star[59]
- A light[60]
- A lamp[61]
- A fire[62]
- A fountain[63]
- A rock[64]
- A shield[65]
- A fortress[66]
- The fountain of life[67]

Poetic Images of Jesus Christ

- Chief Shepherd of the sheep[68]

56. Isa. 53:7.
57. Matt. 23:37.
58. Ps. 84:11.
59. Rev. 22:16.
60. Ps. 27:1.
61. Rev. 21:23.
62. Heb. 12:29.
63. Ps. 36:9.
64. Deut. 32:4.
65. Ps. 84:11.
66. Ps. 46:11.
67. Ps. 36:9.
68. 1 Pet. 5:4.

- Teacher and Lord[69]
- King of kings[70]
- Lord of lords[71]
- Shepherd and Overseer of our souls[72]
- Morning star[73]
- Deliverer[74]
- Advocate[75]
- Second Adam[76]
- Ancient of Days[77]
- Vine[78]
- Chief cornerstone[79]
- Immanuel, God with us[80]
- Firstborn[81]
- Head of the Church[82]
- Physician[83]

69. John 13:13.
70. Rev. 19:16.
71. Rev. 19:16.
72. 1 Pet. 2:25.
73. Rev. 2:28.
74. Rom. 11:26.
75. 1 John 2:1.
76. 1 Cor. 15:45, 47.
77. Dan. 7:13.
78. John 15:5.
79. Eph. 2:20.
80. Isa. 7:14.
81. Rom. 8:29.
82. Col. 1:18.
83. Luke 4:23.

- Rock[84]
- Root of Jesse[85]
- Chief apostle[86]
- Great high priest[87]
- Founder and Perfecter of our faith[88]
- Lamb of God and Lamb slain before the foundation of the world[89]
- Lord God Almighty[90]

We are called to be extremely reverent and to honor the name of God whenever we pray or speak of him. That is why Jesus tells us to start our prayers, "hallowed be your name."[91] Subsequently, it is important that we continually speak to and of God in ways that honor him, are true to his character, and are in accordance with the way in which he reveals himself. Likewise, we should not give him other names or images taken from false religions and spiritualities.

Emotions of God

In addition to the attributes, names, and images of God revealed in Scripture, we also discover the emotions of God in Scripture. This is because God is a person insofar as he is passionate and alive with feelings and thoughts.

84. 1 Cor. 10:4.
85. Rom. 15:12.
86. Heb. 3:1.
87. Heb. 3:1.
88. Heb. 12:2.
89. John 1:36; Rev. 13:8.
90. Rev. 4:8.
91. Matt. 6:9.

When speaking of God's emotions, the Bible is not referring to God being emotional in a pejorative sense, like a young child who is acting nuts because he did not get his nap. When the Bible speaks of the emotions of God, it teaches that the true God is living and passionate. Perhaps the best description of this phenomenon comes from God himself: "The Lord, the Lord, a God merciful and gracious, slow to anger, and abounding in steadfast love and faithfulness, keeping steadfast love for thousands, forgiving iniquity and transgression and sin, but who will by no means clear the guilty, visiting the iniquity of the fathers on the children and the children's children, to the third and the fourth generation."[92] In these two verses, God describes his mercy, grace, patience, love, faithfulness, forgiveness, justice, and anger. Additionally, the Bible speaks of a number of God's emotions, including the following:

- Sorrow[93]
- Anger[94]
- Pleasure[95]
- Jealousy[96]
- Love[97]
- Wrath[98]

92. Ex. 34:6–7.
93. Gen. 6:5–6.
94. Deut. 13:17.
95. Ps. 149:4.
96. Ex. 20:5.
97. 1 John 4:8–10.
98. John 3:36.

- Humor[99]
- Hatred[100]

The Bible also specifically mentions Jesus' emotions, including:
- Anger[101]
- Fear[102]
- Grief[103]
- Sorrow[104]
- Joy[105]
- Compassion[106]
- Love[107]
- Stress[108]

God is not merely the mental concept of many philosophers or the powerful energy or force of paganism. The God revealed in the Bible is passionate and alive. Furthermore, he has made us in his image and likeness to be like him as we live lives filled with healthy and holy expressions of the entire emotional spectrum. Additionally, we more closely connect with our God of emotion when we take our sorrows to him,

99. Ps. 37:13.
100. Ps. 5:5.
101. John 2:14–22.
102. Matt. 26:38–39.
103. John 11:35.
104. Luke 19:41–42.
105. John 15:11.
106. Matt. 9:36; 14:14; 15:32.
107. John 14:31.
108. John 13:21.

express righteous anger over sin, enjoy the pleasures of life in holy ways, remain jealous for those we love, celebrate justice, and hate all that robs God of his glory, whether we are laughing or weeping. We do so because we were created as God's image-bearers, which is the subject of the next section.

In our day, a pagan environmentalism that essentially worships creation as divine often fails to distinguish between human life and animal life. However, the Bible clearly distinguishes between the two without dishonoring creation or the animals, which the man and woman were made to have dominion over and to steward.

Genesis 1:26–28[109] reveals that the reason for human dignity is simply because we were made by God in his image. Additionally, we see that both men and women have equality and dignity because they are both image-bearers of God. One of the results of our image-bearer status is that we possess the shared attributes of God.

Shared Attributes

Unlike the unshared attributes of God, which we examined previously, the shared attributes are those that we as God's image-bearers possess along with God. The difference is that we posses these attributes in a limited way because we are finite creatures, whereas God, our infinite Creator, possesses them in an unlimited way.

109. Cf. James 3:9.

Spirit

God is invisible and immaterial.[110] The Spirit is a person with a mind,[111] emotions,[112] and a will.[113] It is encouraging to know that since we are created in the image and likeness of God, we have a spirit that will live beyond our physical death.

Holiness

God is absolutely separate from any evil.[114] The holiness of God inspires both fear and awe. As God is absolutely holy, it is only through his work that we can come into relationship with him and enter into his presence. We are made holy by his sanctifying work in our lives to make us more and more like Jesus.[115]

Love/Goodness

God alone is perfectly good and loving, and he alone is the source for all goodness and love.[116] All that we do in life should be motivated by our love for God and our neighbor.[117] Because our sins were already punished on Jesus' cross, God is never punishing us, but does discipline us as a loving Father.[118]

110. John 1:18; 3:1–10; 4:19–24; 14:16–17; 16:12–16; 2 Cor. 3:15–17; 1 Tim. 6:15–16.
111. Ps. 139:1–4.
112. Eph. 4:30.
113. John 6:40.
114. Ex. 3:5; Lev. 19:2; Pss. 5:4–6; 99:5; Isa. 6:3; 8:13; 57:15; Hab. 1:12–13; 1 John 1:5; 1 Pet. 1:14–19.
115. 2 Cor. 3:18; 1 Pet. 1:2.
116. Ex. 34:7; Ps. 84:11; John 3:16; Eph. 2:4–7; Gal. 5:22; 1 John 4:8–16.
117. Matt. 22:37–40.
118. Prov. 13:24; Heb. 12:6.

Truth

God is the source and the embodiment of all truth.[119] It brings great confidence and comfort to know we can completely trust God and his Word because he is completely truthful. We too are to be people who believe, speak, and do what is in accordance with the truth.

Justice/Righteousness

God does not conform to a standard of right and wrong, but right and wrong flow out of his character.[120] It is comforting to know God deals fairly with all people, not allowing the guilty to go unpunished, but providing love and mercy to those who turn from sin and to him for forgiveness.

Mercy

God does not give some people what they deserve because he is loving and gracious.[121] Jesus' dying for our sin and saving us from the deserved wrath of God was the ultimate act of mercy for which we should be eternally grateful. Due to his mercy, we should be eagerly merciful to those whom we meet, living as compassionate people who have been given mercy.

Beauty

God is beautiful, and his creation reflects his beauty. God made men and women in his image and likeness to also create works of beauty.[122] In response to God's beauty,

119. Num. 23:19; John 14:6; 17:17; Titus 1:2; 2 Cor. 1:20.
120. Gen. 18:25; Ex. 34:7; Deut. 32:4; Acts 17:31; Rom. 2:11.
121. Ex. 34:6–7; Matt. 18:23–35; Rom. 12:8; Eph. 2:4–7; Titus 3:5.
122. Pss. 27:4; 50:2; Eccles. 3:11; Isa. 33:17.

we should take time to enjoy the beautiful creation he has surrounded us with. We should also appreciate the reflection of his beauty that we find in the arts and creative process, recognizing that creativity is part of being made in the image and likeness of God, an act that gives him glory.

As God's image-bearers who possess his shared attributes, men and women are distinct from and superior to the rest of creation, including animals, which we were created to steward responsibly. As we read the opening chapters of Genesis, we also discover that men and women were created for four relationships. First, we were made to have a spiritual relationship with God. Second, we were made to have a psychological relationship with ourselves. Third, we were made to have social relationships with other people. Fourth, we were made to have an environmental relationship with nature. As a result of our sin, the image and likeness that we bear persists but is marred by sin. Subsequently, as we read the effects of the fall in Scripture and witness its ongoing effects in our world, we see theological problems, psychological problems, social problems, and environmental problems that follow in the wake of sin.

The great theologian Helmut Thielicke (1908–1986) once said that history is in many ways like a good play. When going to a play, one generally asks certain questions such as who wrote the play, who is the hero, who is the villain, and what is the plot. Upon answering these questions, we are able to make sense of and enter into the story in a meaningful way. Likewise, each day people are born onto the stage of history where they will say their lines and act out their part without any concept of who the Author of life is, what great cosmic struggle they find themselves in, who the Hero and Villain are, and how they relate to the plot of which they are a part.

Apart from God's revelation, we are left with meaningless lives in which we seek to either do something significant to be a hero or lose hope and simply accept that we are villains and live according to that brutally despairing truth.

Yet, as we read the Bible, we uncover the source of both our dignity and depravity. As one monk rightly said, we are all angels and demons wrapped up in meat. Indeed, we were made sinless like the angels, but we have descended into the depraved pattern of Satan through sin. Therefore, we are simultaneously both great and wretched, which is the perplexing dilemma of human nature. Those who do not read the Bible and take it to heart are prone to ignore the complex dilemma of our dignity and depravity by favoring one aspect of our nature at the expense of the other. Such people tend to either naively focus solely on the greatness of human potential, or conversely hopelessly focus solely on the greatness of the human potential to do evil.

Genesis 1–2 clearly states that we were made between God and the animals—lower than God but higher than animals. Genesis also states that our position between these two is indeed closer to God than the animals because we bear his image and were handcrafted by him. But those who do not heed the insights of Genesis have the propensity to elevate humans to god-like greatness as the highest and greatest beings, capable of living well and doing good completely in and of our good and glorious selves. Conversely, others are prone to describe us as nothing more than yet another animal, incapable of self-control, beauty, truth, or goodness. An example of the latter is Freud, who essentially reduced us to slaves to our animalistic urges for such things as sex and food.

Genesis alone untangles the great puzzle of our dignity in creation and depravity in sin by pointing us to Jesus, who died for our depravity and rose to redeem us as new creations with our dignity restored. Thankfully, Jesus Christ is our perfect Creator God who humbly entered into human history as a human being. He did so to reveal to us how we are supposed to live and to save us from sin and death so that we can. He will be the subject of our next chapter as our journey toward the truth of God culminates in the incarnation of Jesus Christ.

4

Incarnation of God

Central to the Christian understanding of the revelation of God is the person and work of Jesus Christ. Simply, Christianity is about loving Jesus Christ as God.[1]

Although he is God, Jesus became a human being out of great love, mercy, compassion, and kindness for us. In our sin we have all been separated from God and deserve eternal separation in hell. But God, out of his sheer goodness, came into history as the God-man Jesus Christ. Because he is both God and man, Jesus alone is able to reconcile created, sinful human beings with their holy Creator God. This does not mean that Jesus was a man who became God. Rather, God humbly came down to be a man on the earth, to live, die, and rise so that we could be in a reconciled relationship with God. The Bible describes it this way: "For there is one God, and there is one mediator between God and men, the man Christ Jesus, who

1. For a more in-depth study of the person and work of Jesus Christ, see *Vintage Jesus* by Mark Driscoll and Gerry Breshears (Wheaton, IL: Crossway, 2008).

gave himself as a ransom for all, which is the testimony given at the proper time."[2]

Jesus' life on the earth is commonly referred to by the theological term *incarnation* (from the Latin meaning "becoming flesh").[3] John 1:14 says the Word, the second person of the Trinity, became flesh. John's point is that the eternal, invisible God took on a totally physical body so that we could see him. Our need for this clear revelation of who God is becomes readily apparent when we consider all of the varying, conflicting, and contradictory speculations we examined in the first two chapters of this book.

We will begin by examining the Old Testament promises of Jesus' coming that God spoke through his servants the prophets to announce the incarnation of Jesus. These prophecies are so altogether specific and were so perfectly fulfilled in Jesus that in them we see both that Scripture is from God and that Jesus is God.

Old Testament Prophecies about Jesus' Incarnation

- Seven hundred years before the birth of Jesus, Isaiah promised that Jesus' mother would be a virgin who would conceive by a miracle.[4]
- Seven hundred years before the birth of Jesus, Micah promised that Jesus would be born in Bethlehem.[5]
- Seven hundred years before the birth of Jesus, Hosea promised that Jesus' family would flee as refugees to Egypt to save his young life.[6]

2. 1 Tim. 2:5–6.
3. John 1:14; Phil. 2:5–8; Col. 2:9; 1 John 4:2.
4. Isa. 7:14; Matt. 1:18–23.
5. Mic. 5:2; Luke 2:1–7.
6. Hos. 11:1; Matt. 2:13–15.

- Four hundred years before the birth of Jesus, Malachi promised that Jesus would enter the temple. Since the temple was destroyed in AD 70, this prophecy could not be fulfilled anytime after AD 70.[7]
- Five hundred years before the birth of Jesus, Zechariah promised that Jesus would be betrayed for thirty pieces of silver.[8]
- One thousand years before the birth of Jesus, David promised that lots would be cast for Jesus' clothing.[9]
- One thousand years before the birth of Jesus (and hundreds of years before the invention of crucifixion), David promised that Jesus would be crucified.[10]
- Seven hundred years before the birth of Jesus, Isaiah promised that Jesus would die and be buried in a rich man's tomb.[11]
- One thousand years before the birth of Jesus, David promised that Jesus would resurrect from death;[12] seven hundred years before the birth of Jesus, Isaiah also promised that Jesus would resurrect from death.[13]

In addition to the prophesies that foretold Jesus' coming into history as God become man, Jesus himself repeatedly said he was God. With his proclamation, he refuted the atheists' objection that there is no God, answered the agnostics' befuddlement

7. Mal. 3:1; Luke 2:25–27.
8. Zech. 11:12–13; Matt. 26:14–15.
9. Ps. 22:18; John 19:23–24.
10. Ps. 22:16; Luke 23:33.
11. Isa. 53:8–9; Matt. 27:57–60; Luke 23:46.
12. Ps. 16:10.
13. Isa. 53:10–12; Acts 2:25–32.

that God cannot be known, denied the deists' assertion that God is only distant, contradicted the finite godists' claim that God can do nothing about the pain sin has wrought in our lives, disproved the pantheists' assertion that creation and not Creator is God, negated the panentheists' belief that God is not perfect but still evolving and therefore not ready to be revealed in glory, repudiated the polytheists' postulation that there are many gods, and crushed the monotheists' claim that God is anyone other than the Trinitarian God of the Bible. In light of this, we will now examine the ways in which Jesus repeatedly, clearly, emphatically, and unrelentingly declared himself to be the Only True God.

Jesus' Claims to Deity

Jesus said he came down from heaven. Jesus did not merely say that he had seen heaven, but rather that he had actually come down from heaven where he had previously resided as eternal God: "For I have come down from heaven, not to do my own will but the will of him who sent me."[14] Jesus' claim to be God from heaven is without peer; such a claim has never been made by the founder of any other world religion.

Jesus said he was more than just a good man. In my experience, most people who are not Christians simply think that Jesus was a "good man," but not God. Apparently this idea that Jesus was merely a good guy but not God is nothing new: "And as he [Jesus] was setting out on his journey, a man ran up and knelt before him and asked him, 'Good Teacher, what must I do to inherit eternal life?' And Jesus said to him, 'Why do you call me good? No one is good except God alone.'"[15] This man likely

14. John 6:38.
15. Mark 10:17–18.

thought he was honoring Jesus by calling him a "good teacher." However, Jesus replied that since everyone is a sinner, there is no such thing as a good person—God is the only good person. Jesus was revealing to the man that he was not merely a good person, but in fact God. Even Jesus' enemies were clear that Jesus refused to be considered merely a good man. Those who heard Jesus understood what he was saying and wanted to kill Jesus because he was "making himself equal with God."[16]

Jesus performed miracles. Jesus is emphatic that he did perform miracles and that they helped to prove his claims that he was God. Jesus said, "'Do you say of him whom the Father consecrated and sent into the world, "You are blaspheming," because I said, "I am the Son of God"? If I am not doing the works of my Father, then do not believe me; but if I do them, even though you do not believe me, believe the works, that you may know and understand that the Father is in me and I am in the Father.' Again they sought to arrest him, but he escaped from their hands."[17]

There is ample evidence throughout the New Testament that Jesus performed many miracles. The miracles that Jesus performed were in fact signs pointing to his divinity as he demonstrated his rule over creation as its Creator.

Jesus said he was God. Jesus clearly, emphatically, and repeatedly said he was God. If his statements were untrue, it would have been a blasphemous violation of the First Commandment. Mark 14:61–64 reports, "he remained silent and made no answer. Again the high priest asked him, 'Are you the Christ, the Son of the Blessed?' And Jesus said, 'I am, and you will see the Son of Man seated at the right hand of Power,

16. John 5:18.
17. John 10:36–39.

and coming with the clouds of heaven.' And the high priest tore his garments and said, 'What further witnesses do we need? You have heard his blasphemy. What is your decision?'" John also reports that Jesus said, "I and the Father are one," in response to which "the Jews picked up stones again to stone him. Jesus answered them, 'I have shown you many good works from the Father; for which of them are you going to stone me?' The Jews answered him, 'It is not for a good work that we are going to stone you but for blasphemy, because you, being a man, make yourself God.'"[18]

Throughout the history of the world, numerous people have claimed to speak for God. Yet no leader of any religion has ever claimed to be God. Jesus' claim is simply astonishing. In fact, people kept seeking to kill Jesus for saying it because it would clearly be blasphemy if untrue. Yet, rather than recanting, Jesus died for his claim that he was God.

Jesus said he was sinless. In the history of the world, no one has claimed with any credibility that he is without sin, because to do so is to declare that one's words, actions, thoughts, and motivations are continually perfect and pure. However, Jesus declared that he was not only morally superior to everyone who has ever lived, but in fact sinless. He further challenged anyone to prove him wrong, saying, "Which one of you convicts me of sin? If I tell the truth, why do you not believe me?"[19]

Jesus forgave sin. Many of the resources in our world are spent dealing with the effects of sin (e.g., war, illness, death, depression, crime, poverty). At best, some religions try to

18. John 10:30–33.
19. John 8:46.

teach their adherents what they can do to work hard at paying God back through such things as good works and reincarnation; they still lack any concept of forgiveness.

In light of this, Jesus' claims to forgive sin are simply astonishing. Speaking to a sinful but repentant woman, Jesus said to her, "Your sins are forgiven."[20] Luke 5:20–21 also reports that "when he [Jesus] saw their faith, he said, 'Man, your sins are forgiven you.' And the scribes and the Pharisees began to question, saying, 'Who is this who speaks blasphemies? Who can forgive sins but God alone?'"

Jesus said he was the only way to heaven. Not only did Jesus declare that he came down from heaven, but he also taught that he alone was the only way for anyone to enter into heaven: "I am the way, and the truth, and the life. No one comes to the Father except through me."[21]

In summary, Jesus said he was God come down from heaven to live without sin and forgive our sin so that we might be saved from sin and death and one day be taken to heaven forever. All of this was made possible through Jesus' death and resurrection.

Jesus' Life, Death, Burial, and Resurrection

When we survey the death, evil, and injustice in our world and then hear that this world was made by God, we could rush to one of the false conclusions about God that we examined earlier in this book, such as that there is no God or that God is not powerful, good, or at work in the world. However, the Bible tells us exactly the opposite, namely that God is holy, without any sin, and altogether good. Not only is

20. Luke 7:48.
21. John 14:6.

God good, everything God made was originally good and without sin, including human beings.[22]

Despite the fact that God made us sinless, everyone but Jesus is a sinner both by nature and by choice. Our sin includes our words, deeds, thoughts, and motives. Our sin also includes omission (not doing what God commands) and commission (doing what God forbids).[23]

Sin results in separation from God. Because God is the living God and the source of life, sin results in death. This is similar to a piece of technology being unplugged from its power source; it continues to exist but is functionally dead. In the same way, the Bible says that because of sin we are physically alive but spiritually dead. Furthermore, we will all die physically, just as God promised our first parents in the garden, as a result of our sin against God.[24]

Jesus' Life and Death

To deal with our sin problem and the death it brings, the second member of the Trinity humbly entered into human history.[25] Jesus Christ was tempted just as we are, yet never did sin and therefore lived a perfect life in our place.[26] Despite the greatness of Jesus, sinners put him to death for claiming to be God, which was in fact true.

Two amazingly wonderful things happened on the cross. First, Jesus took our sin upon himself. On the cross as our substitute, Jesus was made to be the worst of what

22. Gen. 1:31; Eccles. 7:29a.
23. Ps. 53:3, 6; Isa. 64:6; Rom. 3:23; 1 John 1:8.
24. Gen. 2:16–17; Rom. 6:23; Eph. 2:1; Col. 2:13.
25. Phil. 2:5–11.
26. Heb. 4:15.

we are. This does not mean that Jesus ever sinned but that he took our sin upon himself. Scripture declares that on the cross, Jesus exchanged his perfection for our imperfection, his obedience for our disobedience, his intimacy with God the Father for our distance from God the Father, his blessing for our curse, and his life for our death. Like Isaiah 53:6 says, "All we like sheep have gone astray; we have turned—every one—to his own way; and the LORD has laid on him the iniquity of us all." Furthermore, "For our sake he made him to be sin who knew no sin, so that in him we might become the righteousness of God."[27]

Second, Jesus died in our place for our sins. The fact that Christians celebrate the murder of Jesus as "good news" and do so every year on "Good Friday" is disgusting unless we understand the reason why Jesus died. The Bible teaches that in perfect justice, because Jesus was made to be our sin, he died for us. The little word *for* has big implications. In theological terms, it means that Jesus' death was substitutionary (or, as some used to call it, vicarious). His death was in our place solely for our benefit and without benefit for himself. Just to be perfectly clear, this means that Jesus took the penalty for our sins in our place so we do not have to suffer the just penalty ourselves. The wrath of God that should have fallen on us and the death that our sins merit fell on Jesus. This wasn't something forced on him. Rather, he took it willingly.[28] Scripture repeatedly stresses this point, which theologians call *penal substitutionary atonement*:

27. 2 Cor. 5:21.
28. John 10:18; Phil. 2:8; Heb. 12:2.

- "But he was wounded *for* our transgressions; he was crushed *for* our iniquities; upon him was the chastisement that brought us peace, and with his stripes we are healed."[29]
- "[He] was delivered up *for* our trespasses. . . ."[30]
- "But God shows his love for us in that while we were still sinners, Christ died *for* us."[31]
- "Christ died *for* our sins. . . ."[32]
- "For Christ also suffered once *for* sins, the righteous *for* the unrighteous, that he might bring us to God. . . ."[33]

Because death is the penalty for sinners, the only way that the death of the sinless Jesus can be understood is in terms of substitution. The sinless Jesus literally stood in our place to suffer and die for us. In doing so, Jesus is our Savior who alone can take away the curse we deserve because of our sin. Not only did Jesus take our sin and death, he also rose from death to conquer sin and death, thereby giving us new life through faith in him. Theologians call this the *doctrine of justification*, which means that guilty sinners can be declared righteous before a holy and righteous God only through faith in Jesus who both takes our sin and gives us his righteousness.[34]

29. Isa. 53:5.
30. Rom. 4:25.
31. Rom. 5:8.
32. 1 Cor. 15:3.
33. 1 Pet. 3:18.
34. Rom. 3:20–27; 2 Cor. 5:21.

Jesus' Burial and Resurrection

Not only did Jesus die, but his body was also wrapped in upwards of one hundred pounds of burial linens and spices before it was laid in a tomb that was sealed with an enormous stone and guarded by a soldier to ensure his body was not stolen. Regarding Jesus' burial, some seven hundred years before Jesus was even born, God promised through Isaiah that Jesus would be assigned a grave "with a rich man in his death."[35] This was incredibly unlikely because Jesus was a very poor man who could not have afforded an expensive burial plot. Yet, following Jesus' death, a wealthy and well-known man named Joseph of Arimathea gifted his expensive tomb for the burial of Jesus.[36] As a result, the place of Jesus' burial was easy to confirm.

Jesus' dead body, however, did not remain in its grave but resurrected in victory over death, fully restored to life. This fact was confirmed after Jesus' resurrection, when many people touched his physical body: his disciples clung to his feet,[37] Mary clung to him,[38] and Thomas the doubter put his hand into the open spear hole in Jesus' side.[39] Jesus appeared to his disciples after his resurrection, but they were uncertain if he had truly physically risen from death. Jesus, however, was emphatic about his bodily resurrection and went out of his way to prove it:

> As they were talking about these things, Jesus himself stood among them, and said to them, "Peace to you!" But they were startled and frightened and thought they saw a spirit. And he said to them, "Why are you troubled, and why do doubts arise in your hearts? See my hands and my feet, that it is I myself. Touch me, and see. For a spirit does not have flesh and bones as you see that I have." And when he had said this, he

35. Isa. 53:9.
36. Matt. 27:57–60.
37. Matt. 28:9.
38. John 20:17.
39. John 20:20–28.

showed them his hands and his feet. And while they still disbelieved for joy and were marveling, he said to them, "Have you anything here to eat?" They gave him a piece of broiled fish, and he took it and ate before them.[40]

Shortly following Jesus' resurrection, Christians began summarizing their doctrinal creeds around Jesus' life, death, burial, and resurrection. For example, Paul says, "Christ died for our sins in accordance with the Scriptures, that he was buried, that he was raised on the third day in accordance with the Scriptures."[41] This statement is widely accepted as the earliest church creed, which began circulating as early as AD 30–36, shortly after Jesus' resurrection. This means that eyewitnesses were still alive to confirm the fact, and there was no time for myth or folklore to emerge about Jesus.

Furthermore, some of the most unlikely people joined in the worship of Jesus after his resurrection because they were eyewitnesses to history's greatest miracle. They include Jesus' own brother James[42] along with Jesus' mother Mary[43] and his other brother Jude.[44]

Perhaps even more shocking was the conversion of a man named Saul, whose name was later changed to Paul. Paul was a devout religious zealot who routinely persecuted and killed Christians.[45] After an encounter with the risen Christ, Paul was converted and became the most dynamic defender and expander of the church.[46] Had Jesus not truly risen from death, it is absurd to assume that Paul would have ever worshiped

40. Luke 24:36–43.
41. 1 Cor. 15:3–4.
42. 1 Cor. 15:7.
43. Acts 1:14.
44. Acts 1:14; Jude 1.
45. Phil. 3:4–6; Acts 7:54–60.
46. Acts 9.

him as God, particularly when Paul rightly believed that worshiping a false God would send one into the eternal flames of hell.

Joining these unlikely converts in the worship of Jesus following his resurrection was a host of other Christians or "little Christs," so named because they wanted to pattern their life and death after Jesus. These people stopped fearing death because they saw that Jesus had defeated it; even in the face of great persecution and martyrdom they did not deny that Jesus alone was God. They began worshiping on Sunday because it was the day Jesus rose, they started partaking of communion to remember Jesus' death through a broken body and shed blood, and they conducted baptisms to show that just as he rose, they too were risen in newness of life cleansed from sin through him. Their eyewitness testimony to the person and work of Jesus was faithfully recorded as the New Testament Scriptures. Through the Scriptures, God the Holy Spirit has birthed a movement of Christians that now includes a few billion people scattered across the various nations and cultures of the earth who worship Jesus alone as God, which is the subject of our next and final chapter.

5

Worship of God

Everyone is a worshiper. God created us to worship; the only difference between people is who they worship and consequently how they worship. Therefore, worship is not something just for religious people, but for all people.

Worship is holding a person or thing in a position of glory and living our lives dedicated to it above all else, as revealed by the sacrifices we make. This connection between glory and worship is clear in verses like Romans 11:36–12:1, which says, "To him be the *glory* forever. Amen. I appeal to you therefore, brothers, by the mercies of God, to present your bodies as a living *sacrifice*, holy and acceptable to God, which is your spiritual *worship*." In this packed section of Scripture, Paul connects a number of vital truths regarding worship.

First, we hold a person or thing in a place of glory. *Glory* means weightiness, importance, preeminence, priority, or that which is our greatest treasure, deepest longing, and fountain of hope. Functionally, what we hold in the place of glory is in effect our real god, despite what our religion might be. For this reason, when people get sick and curse God for not healing them, they are showing that their real God is being healthy, and they value that god above the real God.

Second, we worship that person or thing that we hold in a position of glory. Our worship of that person or thing is done by means of making sacrifices, or dedicating ourselves to that person/thing. In our day, this means that our time, talent, and treasure are given to someone/something rather than the competing options because we hold someone/something as more weighty or glorious than someone/something else.

The opposite of worship is idolatry, or the worship of something or someone other than the One True God of the Bible alone. This theme of worship versus idolatry is in some ways the theme of the entire Bible. Romans articulates the pattern of false worship as failing to glorify God, which leads to an over-inflated and arrogant view of self and ends in worshiping created things rather than the Creator God alone: "For although they knew God, they did not honor him as God or give thanks to him, but they became futile in their thinking, and their foolish hearts were darkened. Claiming to be wise, they became fools, and exchanged the glory of the immortal God for images resembling mortal man and birds and animals and creeping things. Therefore God gave them up in the lusts of their hearts to impurity, to the dishonoring of their bodies among themselves, because they exchanged the truth about God for a lie and worshiped and served the creature rather than the Creator, who is blessed forever! Amen."[1]

At the root of all sin is the pagan confusion, or inversion, of Creator and creation. Indeed, if God is not worshiped then someone/something invariably rises, seeking to sit in his seat of glory. The worship of created things can be either the worship of things God has made, such as the environment or a pet or the human body and the pleasures it gives, or things we have made, such as the television or computer. The result is that a good thing becomes inordinately elevated to a god-thing and therefore a bad thing as we live dedicated to someone/something above God. Often times the

1. Rom. 1:21–25.

god we worship is simply the one we see in the mirror every morning as we brush our teeth.

The biblical word for worship is also sometimes translated "dedication." This insight is helpful because who or what we are dedicated to reveals what we truly live to glorify and worship. In our day, what people wear on their T-shirts, announce on their bumper stickers, write about on their blogs, and link to from their Facebook pages are all telling signs of what they hold in a position of glory. False gods in our day include everything from a boyfriend or girlfriend to a hobby, sport, band, sexual identity, political party, spouse, child, pet, experience, or lifestyle.

The temptation of idolatry is that it proposes a functional savior. What I mean is this. All people have a concept in their mind of what their hell is. They also have a concept in their mind of what their heaven would be. To get out of their proverbial hell and into their desired heaven, they worship a functional savior. While this all sounds very religious and spiritual, in practice it rarely is.

For example, if a young woman sees being single as her hell and dating a cute boy as her heaven, then some guy becomes her functional savior. In dating him she will be taken from her singles' hell into her couples' heaven. The only problem is that she must make sacrifices to worship the boy as a god, such as sleeping with him or putting up with his abuse.

Furthermore, if a man sees chastity before marriage and fidelity in marriage as his hell and naked women as his heaven, then perversion (e.g., porn, fornication, and adultery) becomes his functional savior. The only problem is that he must make sacrifices to worship his false god—blowing massive amounts of time and energy online or at strip clubs and buying cheap drinks for even cheaper women.

The cold, hard truth is not simply that we all worship, but that we also become like that which we worship. For example, if we are dedicated to food we become gluttons, if we are dedicated to drink we become drunkards, and if we are dedicated to comfort we will neglect Christ and his commands to live for God and others in favor of using them for our comfort. As a poignant illustration, the great atheistic philosopher Friedrich Nietzsche not only spent much of his life arguing that God did not exist, but he also spent the final eleven years of his life insane, because when you worship your crazy ideas, you end up crazy.

Foolishly, we do this because we want to have joy, and the advertisements that fill our lives keep promising that if we buy their product, take their pill, join their team, support their cause, vote for their politician, or agree with their worldview then we will be happy. Yet, we remain a bored and depressed multitude because sin only leads to death. Indeed, the worship of anything or anyone other than God is such a great sin that the first two of the Ten Commandments begin by proclaiming that we should only have one God and we should worship that God alone. God said this not to take away our freedom, but rather to give it back so that we might have joy.

Because sin leads to death, idolatry, which is in many ways *the* sin, can never bring the life-giving joy that the worship of God does. Even if sin and the worship of some-one/something other than God is fun for a while, eventually pleasure boomerangs into pain and life becomes dark. Furthermore, when we worship someone/something other than God, we lose perspective and obsession sets in so that we become controlled, mastered, and driven by what we hoped to use for our joy. As a result, we become miserable slaves to our comfort, joy, pride, lust, power, or whatever it was that we chased as a functional savior, only to find that we were lied to by our Enemy who comes to rob, kill, steal, and destroy.

Thankfully, by living as worshipers who continually repent of idolatry and the sins it births, we can have the joy that our hearts long for. After all, it was God who created us with a desire for joy that can only be satisfied in a relationship with him. Sadly, we often choose to satisfy our appetite for our Creator God with created things. As C. S. Lewis poignantly says, "Our Lord finds our desires not too strong, but too weak. We are half-hearted creatures, fooling about with drink and sex and ambition when infinite joy is offered us, like an ignorant child who wants to go on making mud pies in a slum because he cannot imagine what is meant by the offer of a holiday at the sea. We are far too easily pleased."[2]

Therefore, rather than settling for the worship of anyone or anything but the One True God through Jesus our mediator, we must both repent of our idolatries and sins and nurture our passions for glory and joy so that they can only be fulfilled in the worship of God alone. Indeed, we were made by God to worship and will be happy only when we do that for which we were made. My friend Dr. John Piper has stated it this way, "The chief end of man is to glorify God by enjoying Him forever."[3] Saying it another way, he states, "God is most glorified in me when I am most satisfied in Him."[4]

As we near the end of our journey together about the truth of God, the bottom line is that your knowledge about God, perspective about God, understanding of the nature of God, and belief in the incarnation of God are all precursors to your worship of God. Your worship of God is to be done in all of life because it is all sacred; your cubicle at work and kitchen at home are holy places where God dwells with you, just like he did with the Old Testament priests in the Holy of Holies. Anywhere and

2. C. S. Lewis, *The Weight of Glory* (New York: HarperCollins, 2001), 26.
3. John Piper, *Desiring God* (Colorado Springs: Multnomah, 2003), 94.
4. Ibid., 10.

everywhere, you can eat, drink, love, speak, serve, sleep, work, suffer, heal, hurt, laugh, weep, win, lose, repent, live, and die to the glory of God, dedicated to him and worshiping him above all else because in his glory is hidden your joy.

How pathetic it would be if we ended our studies together with stupid religion and mere morality when there is joy at the end of the tether of God's glory. Therefore, I commend to you Jesus Christ—not only as good but the best good—and a new life as a Christian with a new identity, new power, new purpose, new worldview, new passions, new worship, and a new eternity in joy.

Appendix 1

Web Sites for Further Study

This brief book likely raised a number of questions and areas of interest for you. I would strongly encourage you to further your studies on these and other important matters. I have compiled the following list of good and helpful Web sites that include some great articles and referrals of helpful books on a wide variety of Christian topics.

- **www.apologetics.org:** materials on such things as intelligent design and the works of C. S. Lewis.
- **www.apologeticsinfo.org:** a host of brief and solid articles related to the basics of Christianity.
- **www.atlantaapologist.org:** information on everything from cults to basic theology and criticisms of Christian belief.
- **www.carm.org:** a number of articles on Christian doctrine and answers to critics and skeptics.
- **www.equip.org:** a wide number of articles on a host of topics, including the cults, and links to books.
- **www.hisdefense.org:** a host of articles and audio lectures on a wide number of topics.

- **www.kuyper.org:** a Reformed site on cultural engagement.
- **www.origins.org:** a site on creation.
- **www.reasons.org:** a site on creation and issues related to science.
- **www.reformed.org:** Reformed articles on the defense of Christianity.
- **www.wfial.org:** articles on cults and false teachings.

Appendix 2

Books for Further Study

Christians are told to "honor Christ the Lord as holy, always being prepared to make a defense to anyone who asks you for a reason for the hope that is in you; yet do it with gentleness and respect."[1] Simply, Christians are to continually learn and grow in their understanding of their faith so that they may humbly and kindly answer the questions and objections of others regarding Christianity. The branch of Christian study that focuses on equipping people to make just such a defense is called *apologetics,* which means "to make a defense."

This brief book is an introduction to the field of apologetics. I hope it will encourage you to continue your studies. I have compiled the following list of apologetics books that I have benefited from in hopes that some may be of interest and assistance to you.

Answers to Common Questions and Objections

Boa, Kenneth, and Larry Moody. *I'm Glad You Asked.* Colorado Springs: Chariot Victor, 1995.

1. 1 Pet. 3:15–16.

Carroll, Vincent, and David Shiflett. *Christianity on Trial: Arguments against Anti-Religious Bigotry*. San Francisco: Encounter Books, 2002.

Copan, Paul. *How Do You Know You're Not Wrong? Responding to Objections That Leave Christians Speechles*s. Grand Rapids, MI: Baker, 2005.

Craig, William Lane. *Hard Questions, Real Answers*. Wheaton, IL: Crossway, 2003.

Geisler, Norman L., and Ronald Brooks. *When Skeptics Ask: A Handbook on Christian Evidences*. Grand Rapids, MI: Baker, 1990.

Rhodes, Ron. *The Complete Book of Bible Answers: Answering the Tough Questions*. Eugene, OR: Harvest House, 1997.

Rhodes, Ron. *The Truth behind Ghosts, Mediums, and Psychic Phenomena*. Eugene, OR: Harvest House, 2006.

Samples, Kenneth R. *Without a Doubt: Answering the Twenty Toughest Faith Questions*. Grand Rapids, MI: Baker, 2004.

Sampson, Philip J. *Six Modern Myths about Christianity and Western Civilization*. Downers Grove, IL: InterVarsity Press, 2001.

Sproul, R. C. *Reason to Believe: A Response to Common Objections to Christianity*. Grand Rapids, MI: Zondervan, 1982.

Strobel, Lee. *The Case for Faith: A Journalist Investigates the Toughest Objections to Christianity*. Grand Rapids, MI: Zondervan, 2000.

Zacharias, Ravi, and Norman Geisler, eds. *Who Made God? And Answers to Over 100 Other Tough Questions of Faith*. Grand Rapids, MI: Zondervan, 2003.

Apologetics Dictionaries

Geisler, Norman L. *Baker Encyclopedia of Christian Apologetics*. Grand Rapids, MI: Baker, 2006.

McGrath, Gavin, and W. C. Campbell-Jack, eds. *New Dictionary of Christian Apologetics*. Downers Grove, IL: InterVarsity Press, 2006.

Apologetics Introductions

Frame, John M. *Apologetics to the Glory of God: An Introduction*. Phillipsburg, NJ: P&R, 1994.

Geisler, Norman L. *Christian Apologetics*. Grand Rapids, MI: Baker, 1988.

Lewis, C. S. *Mere Christianity*. New York: HarperCollins, 2001.

McGrath, Alister E. *Intellectuals Don't Need God and Other Modern Myths*. Grand Rapids, MI: Zondervan, 1993.

Moreland, J. P. *Scaling the Secular City: A Defense of Christianity*. Grand Rapids, MI: Baker, 1987.

Sproul, R. C. *Defending Your Faith: An Introduction to Apologetics*. Wheaton, IL: Crossway, 2003.

Apologetics Methods

Boa, Kenneth D., and Robert M. Bowman Jr. *Faith Has Its Reasons: An Integrative Approach to Defending Christianity*. Waynesboro, GA: Paternoster, 2006.

Cowan, Steven B., ed. *Five Views on Apologetics*. Grand Rapids, MI: Zondervan, 2000.

Follis, Bryan A. *Truth with Love: The Apologetics of Francis Schaeffer*. Wheaton, IL: Crossway, 2006.

Sproul, R. C., John Gerstner, and Arthur Lindsley. *Classical Apologetics*. Grand Rapids, MI: Zondervan, 1984.

Van Til, Cornelius. *Defense of the Faith*. Phillipsburg, NJ: P&R, 1967.

Atheism

Boa, Kenneth D., and Robert M. Bowman. *Twenty Compelling Evidences That God Exists: Discover Why Believing in God Makes So Much Sense*. Colorado Springs, CO: David C. Cook, 2005.

Geisler, Norman L., and Frank Turek. *I Don't Have Enough Faith to Be an Atheist*. Wheaton, IL: Crossway, 2004.

McGrath, Alister E. *The Twilight of Atheism: The Rise and Fall of Disbelief in the Modern World*. New York: Doubleday, 2004.

McGrath, Alister E., and Joanna Collicutt McGrath. *The Dawkins Delusion? Atheist Fundamentalism and the Denial of the Divine*. Downers Grove, IL: InterVarsity Press, 2007.

Rhodes, Ron. *Answering the Objections of Atheists, Agnostics, and Skeptics*. Eugene, OR: Harvest House, 2006.

Zacharias, Ravi. *Can Man Live without God*. Nashville: Thomas Nelson, 1994.

Zacharias, Ravi. *The Real Face of Atheism*. Grand Rapids, MI: Baker, 2004.

The Bible

Blomberg, Craig L. *The Historical Reliability of the Gospels*. Downers Grove, IL: InterVarsity Press, 2008.

Bruce, F. F. *The Canon of Scripture*. Downers Grove, IL: InterVarsity Press, 1988.

Bruce, F. F. *The New Testament Documents: Are They Reliable?* Downers Grove, IL: InterVarsity Press, 1981.

Cabal, Ted, ed. *The Apologetics Study Bible*. Nashville: Holman, 2007.

Geisler, Norman L., and Thomas Howe. *When Critics Ask: A Popular Handbook on Bible Difficulties*. Grand Rapids, MI: Baker, 1992.

Geisler, Norman L., and William E. Nix. *From God to Us: How We Got Our Bible*. Chicago: Moody, 1974.

Metzger, Bruce M., and Bart D. Ehrman. *The Text of the New Testament: Its Transmission, Corruption, and Restoration*. New York: Oxford University Press, 2005.

Ridderbos, Herman. *The Authority of the New Testament Scriptures*. Grand Rapids, MI: Baker, 1963.

Creation and Evolution

Batten, Don, ed. *The Answers Book: The Twenty Most-Asked Questions about Creation, Evolution, and the Book of Genesis Answered*. Green Forest, AR: New Leaf Press, 1990.

Behe, Michael J. *Darwin's Black Box: The Biochemical Challenge to Evolution*. New York: Free Press, 2006.

Dembski, William A. *The Design Revolution: Answering the Toughest Questions about Intelligent Design*. Downers Grove, IL: InterVarsity Press, 2004.

Dembski, William A. *Intelligent Design: The Bridge between Science and Theology*. Downers Grove, IL: InterVarsity Press, 1999.

Denton, Michael. *Evolution: A Theory in Crisis*. Chevy Chase, MD: Adler & Adler, 1986.

Hagopian, David G., ed. *The Genesis Debate: Three Views on the Days of Creation*. Mission Viejo, CA: Crux Press, 2001.

Johnson, Phillip E. *Darwin on Trial*. Downers Grove, IL: InterVarsity Press, 1993.

Johnson, Phillip E. *Defeating Darwinism by Opening Minds*. Downers Grove, IL: InterVarsity Press, 1997.

McGrath, Alister E. *Dawkins' God: Genes, Memes, and the Meaning of Life*. Malden, MA: Blackwell, 2005.

Moreland, J. P., and John Mark Reynolds, eds. *Three Views on Creation and Evolution*. Grand Rapids, MI: Zondervan, 1999.

Morris, Henry M. *Scientific Creationism*. Green Forest, AR: Master Books, 2000.

Strobel, Lee. *The Case for a Creator: A Journalist Investigates Scientific Evidence That Points Toward God*. Grand Rapids, MI: Zondervan, 2004.

Wells, Jonathan. *Icons of Evolution: Science or Myth? Why Much of What We Teach About Evolution Is Wrong*. Washington, DC: Regnery, 2000.

Witham, Larry A. *By Design: Science and the Search for God*. San Francisco, CA: Encounter Books, 2004.

Witham, Larry A. *Where Darwin Meets the Bible: Creationists and Evolutionists in America*. New York: Oxford University Press, 2002.

Woodward, Thomas. *Doubts about Darwin: A History of Intelligent Design*. Grand Rapids, MI: Baker, 2007.

Cults and World Religions

Enroth, Ronald, ed. *A Guide to New Religious Movements*. Downers Grove, IL: InterVarsity Press, 2005.

Geisler, Norman L., and Ron Rhodes. *Correcting the Cults: Expert Responses to Their Scripture Twisting*. Grand Rapids, MI: Baker, 2005.

Halverson, Dean C., ed. *The Compact Guide to World Religions*. Bloomington, MN: Bethany, 1996.

Martin, Walter. *The Kingdom of the Cults*. Bloomington, MN: Bethany, 2003.

Nichols, Larry A., George A. Mather, and Alvin J. Schmidt. *Encyclopedic Dictionary of Cults, Sects, and World Religions*. Grand Rapids, MI: Zondervan, 2006.

Rhodes, Ron. *The Challenge of the Cults and New Religions*. Grand Rapids, MI: Zondervan, 2001.

Sire, James W. *Scripture Twisting: Twenty Ways the Cults Misread the Bible*. Downers Grove, IL: InterVarsity Press, 1980.

Tennent, Timothy C. *Christianity at the Religious Roundtable: Evangelicalism in Conversation with Hinduism, Buddhism, and Islam*. Grand Rapids, MI: Baker, 2002.

Zacharias, Ravi. *Jesus among Other Gods: The Absolute Claims of the Christian Message*. Nashville: Thomas Nelson, 2002.

Jesus Christ

Habermas, Gary R. *The Historical Jesus: Ancient Evidence for the Life of Christ*. Joplin, MO: College Press, 1996.

Habermas, Gary R., and Michael R. Licona. *The Case for the Resurrection of Jesus*. Grand Rapids, MI: Kregel, 2004.

Strobel, Lee. *The Case for Christ: A Journalist's Personal Investigation of the Evidence for Jesus*. Grand Rapids, MI: Zondervan, 1998.

Strobel, Lee. *The Case for the Real Jesus: A Journalist Investigates Current Attacks on the Identity of Christ*. Grand Rapids, MI: Zondervan, 2007.

Wilkins, Michael J., and J. P. Moreland, eds. *Jesus Under Fire: Modern Scholarship Reinvents the Historical Jesus*. Grand Rapids, MI: Zondervan, 1995.

Miracles

Geisler, Norman L. *Miracles and the Modern Mind: A Defense of Biblical Miracles*. Eugene, OR: Wipf & Stock, 2004.

Lewis, C. S. *Miracles*. New York: HarperCollins, 2001.

New Age

Clifford, Ross, and Phillip Johnson. *Jesus and the Gods of the New Age*. Colorado Springs, CO: Victor, 2003.

Miller, Elliot. *A Crash Course on the New Age Movement*. Grand Rapids, MI: Baker, 1989.

Rhodes, Ron. *The Counterfeit Christ of the New Age Movement*. Grand Rapids, MI: Baker, 1991.

Rhodes, Ron. *New Age Movement*. Grand Rapids, MI: Zondervan, 1995.

Philosophers and Philosophies

DeWeese, Garrett J., and J. P. Moreland. *Philosophy Made Slightly Less Difficult: A Beginner's Guide to Life's Big Questions*. Downers Grove, IL: InterVarsity Press, 2005.

Geisler, Norman L., and Paul D. Feinberg. *Introduction to Philosophy: A Christian Perspective*. Grand Rapids, MI: Baker, 1987.

Wilkens, Steve. *Good Ideas from Questionable Christians and Outright Pagans: An Introduction to Key Thinkers and Philosophies.* Downers Grove, IL: InterVarsity Press, 2004.

Postmodernism

Grenz, Stanley J. *A Primer on Postmodernism.* Grand Rapids, MI: Eerdmans, 1996.

Penner, Myron B., ed. *Christianity and the Postmodern Turn: Six Views.* Grand Rapids, MI: Brazos Press, 2005.

Smith, James K. A. *Who's Afraid of Postmodernism? Taking Derrida, Lyotard, and Foucault to Church.* Grand Rapids, MI: Baker, 2006.

Wells, David F. *Above All Earthly Pow'rs: Christ in a Postmodern World.* Grand Rapids, MI: Eerdmans, 2005.

Pluralism

Newbigin, Lesslie. *The Gospel in a Pluralist Society.* Grand Rapids, MI: Eerdmans, 1989.

Okholm, Dennis L., and Timothy R. Phillips, eds. *Four Views on Salvation in a Pluralistic World.* Grand Rapids, MI: Zondervan, 1996.

Phillips, Richard, ed. *Only One Way? Reaffirming the Exclusive Truth Claims of Christianity.* Wheaton, IL: Crossway, 2006.

The Problem of Evil

Feinberg, John S. *The Many Faces of Evil: Theological Systems and the Problems of Evil.* Wheaton, IL: Crossway, 2004.

Lewis, C. S. *The Problem of Pain.* New York: HarperCollins, 1996.

Plantinga, Alvin. *God, Freedom, and Evil.* Grand Rapids, MI: Eerdmans, 2001.

Relativism

Beckwith, Francis J., and Gregory Koukl. *Relativism: Feet Firmly Planted in Mid-Air*. Grand Rapids, MI: Baker, 1998.

Science

Colson, Charles W., and Nancy Pearcey. *Science and Evolution: Developing a Christian Worldview of Science and Evolution*. Wheaton, IL: Tyndale, 2001.

Johnson, Phillip E. *Reason in the Balance: The Case against Naturalism in Science, Law, and Education*. Downers Grove, IL: InterVarsity Press, 1995.

Johnson, Phillip E. *The Wedge of Truth: Splitting the Foundations of Naturalism*. Downers Grove, IL: InterVarsity Press, 2002.

McGrath, Alister E. *The Science of God: An Introduction to Scientific Theology*. Grand Rapids, MI: Eerdmans, 2004.

Miller, Kenneth R. *Finding Darwin's God: A Scientist's Search for Common Ground Between God and Evolution*. New York: HarperCollins, 2007.

Moreland, J. P. *Christianity and the Nature of Science*. Grand Rapids, MI: Baker, 1999.

Morris, Henry M. *The Biblical Basis for Modern Science*. Green Forest, AR: Master Books, 2002.

Ross, Hugh. *Beyond the Cosmos*. Colorado Springs, CO: NavPress, 1999.

Ross, Hugh. *The Creator and the Cosmos: How the Latest Scientific Discoveries of the Century Reveal God*. Colorado Springs, CO: NavPress, 2001.

Ross, Hugh. *The Genesis Question: Scientific Advances and the Accuracy of Genesis*. Colorado Springs, CO: NavPress, 2001.

Schroeder, Gerald. *Genesis and the Big Bang: The Discovery of Harmony between Modern Science and the Bible*. New York: Bantam, 1992.

Worldviews

Sire, James W. *The Universe Next Door: A Basic Worldview Catalog.* Downers Grove, IL: InterVarsity Press, 1997.

Sproul, R. C. *Lifeviews*. Grand Rapids, MI: Revell, 2000.

Pastor Mark Driscoll founded Mars Hill Church (www.marshillchurch.org) in Seattle in the fall of 1996, which has grown to over six thousand people in one of America's least churched cities. He co-founded and is president of the Acts 29 Church Planting Network (www.acts29network.org), which has planted over one hundred churches in the United States and internationally. Most recently he founded the Resurgence Missional Theology Cooperative (www.theresurgence.com).

Outreach magazine has recognized Mars Hill Church as the second most innovative, twenty-third fastest-growing, and second most prolific church-planting church in America. *The Church Report* has recognized Pastor Mark as the eighth most influential pastor in America. His sermons are downloaded a few million times a year. *Seattle* magazine has named Pastor Mark one of the twenty-five most powerful people in Seattle.

Media coverage on Pastor Mark and Mars Hill varies from National Public Radio to *Mother Jones* magazine, the *Associated Press*, the *New York Times*, *Blender* music magazine, *Outreach* magazine, *Christianity Today*, *Preaching Today*, and *Leadership* magazine to ABC Television and the 700 Club.

His writing includes the books *Vintage Jesus, The Radical Reformission: Reaching Out without Selling Out,* and *Confessions of a Reformission Rev.: Hard Lessons from an Emerging Missional Church*. He also contributed to the books *The Supremacy of Christ in a Postmodern World* and *Listening to the Beliefs of Emerging Churches*. Most enjoyably, Mark and his high school sweetheart, Grace, delight in raising their three sons and two daughters.